In this insightful volume Herbert London lays bare the assumptions behind the new faith of secularism and the challenge this doctrine poses to America's traditional ideals of self government, patriotism, and national strength. Mr. London presents clear answers to the troubling questions he poses. *America's Secular Challenge* deserves to be read by Americans of all faiths.

JAMES PIERESON
Senior Fellow, The Manhattan Institute

America's Secular Challenge is the widow's curse of moral and political philosophy. Because it is a book of modest length, it ought logically to contain only a modest amount of wisdom and commonsense. Yet because it draws on the accumulated experience both of the Judaeo-Christian religious tradition and of the Anglo-American political tradition of ordered liberty, there is for practical purposes an infinite amount of wisdom and commonsense in its pages. However much you take out, somehow there's always a little more left—on for example the real meaning of tolerance or the necessity of patriotism. You simply have to turn the page.

JOHN O'SULLIVAN

I suspected there was something amiss with the secular humanist purrings, and now Herbert London has made it all very clear with wide learning and deep insight for which I am grateful. This is an essential book.

R. EMMETT TYRRELL, JR.
Founder and Editor in Chief, The American Spectator

Political religion first emerged out of the cauldron of the French Revolution as Jacobinism. In his short but compelling book Herbert London shows that today's militant secularists are, in their own way, the heirs of the Jacobins— but with a difference. While the Jacobins had a positive, as they saw it, program; today's militant secularists are merely negative. But, as London shows, their hostility to the values underlying American life, at time when they are under attack from radical Islam, represents a threat we shouldn't underestimate.

FRED SIEGEL
The Cooper Union for Science and Art

With wisdom distilled by a lifetime's engagement with ideas that matter, Herb London offers a compelling invitation to believe again in truths upon which our future depends.

REV. RICHARD JOHN NEUHAUS
Editor in Chief, First Things

AMERICA'S SECULAR CHALLENGE

BOOKS BY HERBERT LONDON

Non-White Immigration and the White Australia Policy
Fitting In: Crosswise At Generation Gap
The Overheated Decade
The Seventies: Counterfeit Decade
Myths That Rule America (written with Al Weeks)
Military Doctrine and The American Character:
        Reflections on Air Land Battle
Why Are They Lying To Our Children?
Closing The Circle: A Cultural History of
        The Rock Revolution
Armageddon In The Classroom: An Examination
        of Nuclear Education
The Broken Apple: New York City in the 1980's
From The Empire State to The Vampire State:
        New York in a Downward Transition
        (written with Edwin Rubenstein)
Decade of Denial: A Snapshot of America in the 1990's
A Roadmap for Japan's Future
        (written with Kenneth Weinstein)

America's Secular Challenge

The Rise of a New
National Religion

HERBERT LONDON

BRIEF ENCOUNTERS
Encounter Books · New York · London

Copyright © 2008 by Herbert London

First edition published in 2008 by Encounter Books,
an activity of Encounter for Culture and Education, Inc.,
a nonprofit, tax exempt corporation.

Encounter Books website address: *www.encounterbooks.com*

Manufactured in the United States and printed on acid-free paper.
The paper used in this publication meets the minimum requirements of
ANSI/NISO Z39.48−1992 (R 1997) (Permanence of Paper).

FIRST EDITION

LIBRARY OF CONGRESS CATALOGING-IN-PUBLICATION DATA

London, Herbert Ira.
America's secular challenge : the rise of a new national religion /
by Herbert London.
    p.   cm. — (Brief encounters)
Includes index.
ISBN-13: 978-1-59403-227-1 (hardcover : alk. paper)
ISBN-10: 1-59403-227-0 (hardcover : alk. paper)
1. United States—Religion. I. Title.
BL2525.L66   2008
200.973'0905—dc22
2008001922

10 9 8 7 6 5 4 3 2 1

Contents

Preface 1

Introduction 3

CHAPTER 1   Secularism: America's New Religion 11

CHAPTER 2   Truth as a Relative Concept 25

CHAPTER 3   The Limitations of Science 33

CHAPTER 4   Government's Rationalist Largesse 42

CHAPTER 5   Patriotism as a Moral Problem 52

CHAPTER 6   Tolerance, Discrimination, and
             Discernment 66

Conclusion 81

Acknowledgments 99

Index 101

To my wife Vicki and my three daughters
Stacy, Nancy and Jaclyn

Preface

BELIEF MATTERS. In this short book, I hope to under-score the truth of that simple statement. In particular, I hope to demonstrate that our culture's increasing commitment to the tenets of radical secularism undermines our resolve to oppose a fanatical foe on the world stage.

This is not, I am well aware, an idea that enjoys much credence among the liberal elite, many of whom distrust religious belief of any kind. Yet the question is whether radical secularism offers a sufficiently robust alternative to religion—robust enough, that is, to nurture our allegiance to the core values of Western civilization at a time when those values are under siege not only from the external threat of radical Islam but also from the internal threats of spiritual fecklessness and moral anemia. Robert Frost once said that a liberal was someone who refused to take his own side in an argument. Radical secularism, bolstered by the relativistic teachings of multiculturalism, elevates that foible into a philosophy of life.

What this book attempts to do is identify the defining characteristics of that philosophy and provide an anatomy of its influence on American culture. Opposition to traditional religion; multiculturalism and cultural relativism; unbridled sexual expression; materialism; economic egalitarianism; belief in scientific rationality as the ultimate arbiter of human

Preface

value: Taken together, I believe, these features of the secularist's creed underwrite a view of life ill-equipped to meet
the political and existential challenges of the twenty-first
century. The nature of that creed and the character of those
challenges form the subject of this book.

Introduction

Things fall apart; the centre cannot hold;
Mere anarchy is loosed upon the world,
The blood-dimmed tide is loosed, and everywhere
The ceremony of innocence is drowned;
The best lack all conviction, while the worst
Are full of passionate intensity.
—W. B. Yeats, "The Second Coming"

GREAT CHANGES are afoot in Western culture. The world as we've known it is becoming a markedly different place, and a more dangerous one, where the very basis of our civilization is increasingly challenged. Let me begin by identifying some of the intellectual and moral factors that are altering our cultural landscape.

The first is multiculturalism, an attitude that proclaims the equality of all cultures but paradoxically assumes that non-Western cultures are somehow more equal, more worthy, than their Western counterparts. This Orwellian phenomenon preaches the gospel of equality, but proceeds as much from self-loathing as from egalitarianism. If women in America on average earn less than men, that is a form of oppression; but if an African culture indulges in ritual mutilation in the form of clitoridectomy, that, for the multiculturalist, is simply an expression of cultural difference.

A second factor precipitating cultural change in the West is the decay of religion. European churches are now more museums than places of worship. And even the much-touted

Introduction

In 1954 President Eisenhower, not typically remembered for his Christian observance, said, "Our government makes no sense unless it is founded on deeply religious faith and I don't care what it is." This may be a reflection of Eisenhower's Erasmian view of religion as something taking its force more from commitment to moral conduct than from theological dogma. Even so, Eisenhower here was suggesting something unique about faith in the public service.

Of course, faith comes in many forms. Secularism itself is a kind of faith, as is the dogmatic commitment to scientific rationality, to which so many secularists appeal in the hopes of answering moral and ontological questions that were once answered by religion. Even what the sociologist Robert Bellah, and Rousseau before him, called "civil religion" involves faith in the achievements and existential vitality of our republican traditions, including its religious traditions.

For the secular humanist, the fact that the mass of humanity may be unable to live without religion is not dispositive. In considering this matter, however, the secularist disinters a "religious" canon of his own, one that has a distinct value system even as it rejects Christianity and Judaism. Of course, the secularist challenge to religion has been an important social force since the Enlightenment. What is different today is the unwitting collusion between some of the attitudes fostered by secularism and those promoted by the enemies of the West. As Bernard Lewis, a great scholar of Islam, and others have observed, democracies around the world face an imminent danger from elements within their own societies that often pose as pro-peace and human rights. In the West, the leftist naïveté that exaggerates the imperfections in democracy has fueled the Islamic agenda that challenges the West.

It has become increasingly obvious that, like it or not, the West is locked in a civilizational struggle with radical Islam. According to Norman Podhoretz, we are already engaged in World War IV (World War III having been the decades-long Cold War). As the first decade of the twenty-first century comes to a close, it seems clear that there will either be a rebirth of the West, bolstered by a resuscitation of its key traditions, or further disintegration as we struggle ineptly against fanaticism. As Mark Steyn has shown in *America Alone*, the startling demographic decline of Europe and Russia—the birthrate in Europe as a whole is 1.38 percent, significantly below "replacement" level—all but assures a showdown with rapidly multiplying Islamic populations. Meanwhile, the strategy of Islamists is clear: destroy Israel, create a Middle East devoid of any religion but Islam, employ the oil empire to create caliphates from Madrid to Jakarta and then launch a holy war against the West. What remains to be seen is whether such a philosophy would face any real opposition by a weakened West in the decades to come.

In this struggle America is perceived as the Great Satan, not merely by enemies such as Osama bin Laden and al Qaeda, but by supposed allies in Egypt and western Europe. For example, Egyptian MP Mustafa Zakri recently opined that "America is the head of the serpent, and the greatest enemy, which we must confront."

The root of this enmity is centuries old: Some trace it to the victory of Charles Martel at the Battle of Tours in 732. It is not coincidental that Sheik Nasrallah, leader of Hezbollah, continually makes reference to the history of Saladin and refers to the United States and Israel as "crusaders." Yet there is a nagging question: Why now? Why were there coordinated, violent demonstrations across the globe over cartoons that caricatured the prophet Mohammed? Why is every real or perceived slight against Islam exaggerated into a *casus belli*? After all, in the *Divine Comedy*, Dante meets Mohammed suffering in the fires of hell. The Cathedral of Bologna has shown frescoes of Mohammed seen in an unfavorable light for hundreds of years.

Certainly part of the reason for the recent tumult is the belief circulating in the Islamic world that a secular West no longer has the will to resist Islamic jihad. The compromises and willingness to accommodate Islamic factions in European societies are interpreted as signs of weakness. The more open and liberal the society, the more likely it is a target for jihad. It was no accident, as the Marxists used to say, that Denmark and Holland, two of the most radically secular countries in Europe, should have been the site of some of the most violent Islamic outrages in recent years: in Denmark, the destructive riots that exploded in the aftermath of the publication of cartoon caricatures of Mohammed in the *Jyllands-Posten*; in Holland, the grisly murder of the filmmaker Theo van Gogh on the streets of Amsterdam.

For Islamists, the moment for a triumphalist campaign has arrived, a moment not unlike the jihad Mohammed launched against the three Jewish tribes in Arabia in the seventh century. That the West considers this Islamic fanaticism a form of acting out over deplorable conditions faced by Muslims within their own borders also plays to Islam's strength. Believing that there must be a rational explanation for seemingly irrational behavior, Western leaders and opinion makers bend over backwards to contrive exculpatory explanations. Rarely do they come to the conclusion that the violence is fomented by religious zealotry no liberal concessions can possibly mitigate.

The riots that attend every minor offense are aimed at breaking Western will. They are a tactic to test the fortitude of the West, to see if there is any devotion that can withstand the onslaught. If one were to consider the feeble response from European capitals, one would have to conclude that the Islamic clerics are right. Rather than treat the riots as a frontal attack on the West, most leaders describe the incidents as aberrations, a function of high unemployment rates or poor housing conditions.

Consider the incendiary pronouncements of the Iranian president Mahmoud Ahmadinejad, who has repeatedly promised to "wipe Israel off the map." Many commentators in the West discount Ahmadinejad's rhetoric as a form of propaganda that should not be taken too seriously. But why not? Liberal *bien pensants* took the same tack with Hitler in the 1930s, ignoring or rationalizing his extreme pronouncements as the unfortunate but mostly harmless rantings of a madman. We all know what the fruits of their appeasement were. It is the same with Ahmadinejad. His call for martyrdom is a plea for Armageddon. What he says is precisely what he and the mullahs believe.

There is a civilizational fatwa metastasizing around the globe, from Hamburg to Tehran, from Nablus to Malmö, from Copenhagen to Islamabad. For Muslims, jihad is in the air and the more it manifests itself in orchestrated street theater, the more it will highlight the weakness of the West.

Introduction

The confrontation between radical Islam and the West is fast becoming the defining test of our age. How that contest unfolds remains to be seen. But if the West cannot marshal the strength to defend its core values, these contemporary Crusades will assuredly end in disaster. Part—a large part, in fact—of that task is spiritual. It involves challenging the gospel of radical secularism, according to which the goal of human life is entirely defined by material well-being.

What the political philosopher James Burnham observed about the West's confrontation with Communism is even truer with respect to its confrontation with radical Islam. "No one," Burnham wrote, "is willing to sacrifice and die for progressive education, Medicare, humanity in the abstract, the United Nations, and a ten percent rise in Social Security payments." And yet such "bloodless abstractions" essentially exhaust what secularism has on offer. "Things fall apart," Yeats wrote in his famous poem, "the centre cannot hold." It is not yet certain whether Yeats's dour vision is more a news report or a warning. I believe that we still command the resources to salvage the spiritual center of our civilization. But to accomplish this we must have the courage to challenge the seductive tenets of radical secularism and revivify the traditional values that informed and nourished America. This book is a contribution to that task.

1 | Secularism: America's New Religion

"Everyone is more or less mad on one point"
—Rudyard Kipling, *On The Strength of Likeness*

IF AMERICA'S secular humanists can be said to have a particular goal in mind, it is the wholesale removal of religion from public life. Secularists frequently cast themselves as defenders of the separation of church and state, but what they argue for is in fact something more comprehensive: that religious observance and even religious principles be relegated to the private thoughts of the faithful.

So much of American society has been constructed on the basis of both the belief in the divine and the organizational religion that it entails that secularism threatens to leave America with a "naked public square," to borrow a phrase from Father Richard Neuhaus. Secularists justify their anti-religious sentiments by citing concerns about the impending "theocracy" of the Religious Right. This is odd, because in many respects secularism is itself not unlike a religion. It is grounded in several ideas that are valued by its adherents as deeply and unquestioningly as any spiritual creed.

One of these ideas is that truth is relative—that is, contextual. That some truths may be divinely ordained and therefore universally applicable is regarded as simplistic, naïve, or worse. If a particular moral position is to one's benefit, it may be considered "valid," however it offends traditional morality. All judgment becomes a function of pragmatism: If it works for me, it must be true. Overarching moral considerations emanating from natural law or even historical antecedents take a back seat to personal choice.

The secularist doctrine discards the notion that truth and knowledge consist of the humane teachings of two millennia of Judeo-Christian philosophy; it accepts only what may be ascertained and tested by scientific inquiry. Whatever cannot be proven or measured or is in some sense intangible is not worthy of consideration. We know that magnetism, electricity, and gravity exist, because science has shown that to be the case. We do not know that God "exists" in any material sense. But must that mean that God—to say nothing of a host of other matters beyond our present understanding—doesn't count? For the secularist, the answer is an emphatic "yes."

A believer in God knows enough to know that he doesn't know anything for certain. A nonbeliever says that no concrete proof of God can exist, and therefore God *cannot* exist. For the secularist, the matter is entirely closed. Which position, in the end, is the more unbending one?

The wages of this self-satisfied conviction are a loss of the glue that provides social cohesion. A moral code that is regarded as proceeding not from God but from human reason will always be subject to change. What seems obvious to "reasonable" people of one generation may be jettisoned the instant it becomes inconvenient. As it happens, "reasonable" and "convenient" are nowadays frequently used interchangeably.

In a significant conflict between reason and faith, fought in a society predicated on science, reason will generally triumph. Consider the controversy surrounding Theresa Schiavo, the brain-damaged woman whose feeding tube was removed in March, 2005. Her parents had long clung to the faith that she was alive, even that she might recover, despite the medical community's declaration that she was in a "persistent vegetative state," essentially dead without life support systems. Notwithstanding what one thinks of the subsequent political charade, in the first instance the imperatives of faith were subordinated to law and medical opinion.

Notwithstanding the claim that Americans share a common culture, there is now a fundamental discord in the land, which becomes increasingly evident in light of events like the Schiavo controversy. It was evident, too, when newspapers of record argued that President George W. Bush's success in the 2004 election was due primarily to the outpouring of support from the evangelical Christian community. One could detect a subtext in this parsing of the election results, that evangelicals' support was somehow an unfair advantage, predicated on concerns of faith that have no place in the political sphere. It was as if the votes of credulous evangelicals didn't mean much, even though they regularly prove to be more informed on "the issues" than, say, urban voters who overwhelmingly cast ballots for Democrats.

In spite of this discord, it is worth asking whether the majority of Americans wants religion excluded from every corner of public life. Despite the secular sentiments of many members of the intellectual and cultural elite, most Americans profess belief in God. Nevertheless, there is a powerful campaign underway to suppress religious expression. Individuals may pray and sing hymns in private, so as not to give offense to nonbelievers, but such limitations transform religious observance into something shameful. Religion cannot long endure if it is seen as such—a fact of which the secularists cannot possibly be unaware.

Herbert London

Of course, ours is a nation founded by men who understood that religion, far from being an embarrassment, is a valuable and sustaining aspect of individual—and national —character. It was so important to the founding fathers that they addressed it in the First Amendment to the Constitution, which states that Congress cannot make any laws "prohibiting the free exercise" of religion. Nearly any religious practice is permitted—whenever, wherever, and by anyone.

The other part of the First Amendment that touches on religion—prohibiting the "establishment of religion"—was originally construed as preventing the establishment of a particular state religion like Britain's Anglicanism. But now, the Supreme Court has given itself the task of ensuring that the so-called "Establishment Clause" supersedes the more fundamental "Free Exercise Clause." In other words: If religion isn't violating the law, the law will just have to be changed.

There is some political opposition to this process. Tim Kaine, the governor of Virginia and both a Democrat and a Catholic, remarked, "We can't completely separate politics and faith. They rise from the same wellspring: the concern about the distance between what is and what ought to be." This is a useful point to keep in mind. Secularism is in its own way about the distance between what is and what ought to be, though on a far smaller and more personal scale. It's not for nothing that the pursuits of financial success and material goods have become rituals of an almost religious character. Surely secularists would never acknowledge this, but there it is: Life is about bridging the gap between oneself and what one would like to become, whether it's rich, beautiful, enviable, or "self-actualized" in some abstract but no less potent sense.

In the late 1960s, a belief began to emerge that the existence of God meant the existence of unfair and superfluous constraints on personal freedom. Why live to fulfill "God's plan" when one has plenty of plans of his own? The selfishness of these secularists, aptly called the "me generation," consisted mainly of new-age pretensions of "self-knowledge," a cloak, essentially, for the relentless fulfillment of personal wishes.

Not surprisingly, the idea that man's search for meaning can be satisfied by getting in touch with one's feelings became something of a cottage industry. Canny gurus and speakers made millions writing books and delivering seminars on this topic, all in the guise of ushering in the "new age." At first glance, such seminars resembled church services: a preacher speaking to his congregation about the sorts of beliefs and behaviors likely to lead to contentment—salvation in the temporal sense. The critical difference between religious and secular leaders, of course, is that the former believe in a higher power, while the latter believes that man is the highest power. It isn't difficult to see the appeal this held for an entire generation of Americans, and it sadly continues today. Rhonda Byrne's self-help book *The Secret* is premised on the fantasy that a person can simply will whatever he wants—money, a new car, a girlfriend—into his life; this claptrap has sold, as of writing, over three million copies.

The notion that God's existence, taken as fact, limits mankind's freedom did not spring fully formed from the 1960s. Jean-Jacques Rousseau, for example, argued that liberty demands the abolition of all dependencies, whether upon God or upon the family. But as the founding fathers of this nation fully understood, without such alliances—without, that is, the powerful mediating structures of family and church—the social contract cannot exist.

The Rousseauian vision haunts contemporary America. The lineaments of social organization continue to face a number of challenges. Proponents of gay marriage push their agenda without giving a worthy reply to the argument that they are contributing to the idea that mores and behaviors are arbitrary. Why stop to wonder what purpose was served by the old ideal of marriage? It is merely smeared with the charge of "discrimination," an unacceptable social and legal evil in our day. But if the part of the definition of marriage that specifies it as a covenant between a man and a woman is discriminatory, why isn't the part that defines it as between two people likewise discriminatory? Gay-rights activism on this point only goes to demonstrate the true *modus operandi* of modern interest-group politics: We want what we want, and with enough pressure, we'll get it sooner rather than later. The same goes for advocates of late-term or partial-birth abortion: That what they defend is better described as infanticide is only a small and easily dismissed impediment to their radical view of "personal freedom." "Freedom to be me" has evolved—or, to put it more properly, devolved—from the sublime of Ayn Rand's heroes to the absurdity of the Yippies who took for their slogan, "If it feels good, do it."

Though many of the self-centered beliefs of modern secularists have their roots in the eighteenth and nineteenth centuries, they experienced a powerful and influential revival and reformulation during the 1960s and 1970s. Due in part to the Vietnam War, many young people became suspicious of all authority, of anyone who told them what to do or believe. The military draft, needless to say, became the focus of this discontent. What is perhaps more surprising is that the Baby Boom generation grouped religious institutions with the government and military. These groups together made up the detested "Establishment."

Characterizing organized religion as part of the same "Establishment" that included the military-industrial complex was certainly a stretch. Many clergymen, such as Martin Luther King, Jr., had strongly denounced the Kennedy and Johnson administrations for prolonging the Vietnam War, and had advocated for peace, equal rights, and new measures to end poverty. Nevertheless, religion was regarded by the young as yet another imposition of limits to behavior, a burden that impeded the pursuit of happiness. The popular belief at the time—which prevails today despite the massive emotional and social damage it has wrought—was that anything that limits personal freedom is wrong.

The Mamas and the Papas sang "go where you want to go, do what you want to do" to a generation that rejected constraints of any kind. But having chosen limitless freedom for oneself, why preach it to others? One explanation is that people sometimes tolerate the behavior of others because they want their own self-centered behavior to be tolerated in turn. Tolerance has its place, but this kind of *quid pro quo* quickly becomes dangerous: Behavior is tolerated without the least regard for judgment, taste, or virtue. Social attitudes may be expected to change with the times, but the capacity for judgment may simply vanish if judgment—of

17

one's own behavior, and of others'—is never exercised. The question for a tolerant society is: At what point does tolerance cross over into mere moral anarchy?

In George Orwell's *1984*, the torturer O'Brien tells Winston Smith that, "You are imagining that there is something called human nature which will be outraged by what we do and will turn against us. But we create human nature. Men are infinitely malleable." Indeed, governments unrestrained by religious belief generally try the hardest, and with the bloodiest results, to shape human nature. But while man is malleable, he is certainly not infinitely malleable. There are limits to what his nature can accept without being destroyed.

Religion has historically acted as a guidepost for man, a reminder that there are times to be tolerant and times to distinguish evil from good and choose the latter. Religion is also the most potent antidote to solipsism and its attendant "morality of me." In 1970, Jerry Rubin published *Do It!—Scenarios of the Revolution*, a book which, as its title suggests, encouraged readers to eschew all behavioral restraints in pursuit of the "revolution." Needless to say, just "doing" is not the same as doing good. A society whose members are interested only in their own "self-actualization," be it through personal gratification or the pursuit of some nebulous "revolution," cannot really be called a society at all.

Similarly, a culture willing to accept the accumulation of wealth as its greatest good will ultimately destroy itself. Wilhelm Roepke, a leading free-market economist, wrote that "the market does not create values, but consumes them and it must be constantly reimpregnated against rot." The choice before Americans is between reimpregnation with core values and the passive acceptance of incremental rot.

One can believe in the values that spring from religion or the values of materialism, but not both. Adam Smith, the author of *The Wealth of Nations* and sometimes described as the father of the free-market system, was also a distinctively moral philosopher, the author of *The Theory of Moral Sentiments*. He recognized that a free market unfettered by moral principles ultimately will prove corrosive to society. The disposition to improve oneself, Smith wrote, while essential to economic health, is also "the great and most universal cause" of the "corruption of our moral sentiments."

Free-market capitalism, in its purest form, imposes no prohibitions on economic activity. Slavery, prostitution, and the drug trade are permissible, even encouraged, as they allow for the creation of wealth. We do not practice such a system, however, because it would be destructive not only to itself but to individual lives. Little was restrained or forbidden in the decadent years of late imperial Rome; citizens could indulge every physical desire to their heart's content. As history shows us, this kind of society cannot defend itself against outside forces. As Arnold Toynbee once noted, societies die not by murder but by suicide.

Robert Browning wrote in "Pippa Passes," "God's in His heaven—/ All's right with the world." Well, all may not be right, but were God not in His heaven all would certainly be wrong. The world and human behavior are not, of course, perfectible, but without religious belief they become infinitely corruptible. Because they rely on divine origins, nearly all religions tout an ethics external to and above any one man and his whims. In this way, organized religion reinforces the law, and encourages societies to police themselves.

The importance of this ameliorating effect on human

society cannot be overstated, but intellectuals and sophisti-
cates have long scoffed at religious observance, contending
that it is sheer pretense. They ought to keep in mind Evelyn
Waugh's famous response to a woman who asked him how,
given all of the vicious things he wrote, said, and did, he
could consider himself a Christian: "Madam, I may be all
the things you say. But believe me, were it not for my religion, I would scarcely be a human being."

Even while rejecting the dogmas of others, secularists
fail to see that their own worldview is dogmatic in character. Secularists are reluctant to question the values of personal transformation and immediate gratification. Let us
examine seven articles of a possible secularist catechism:

— Truth is subjective, relative, or contextual. That
there may exist objective spiritual truths is rejected
as the product of naïve or inflexible minds.

— Rationality can solve moral and ontological questions about man's nature. The Thomistic faith that
inspires wisdom is rejected as a mere fairytale. Only
science can reveal knowledge.

— A rational government is freed from the limits tra-
ditionally imposed on its purview through the attain-
ment of technical knowledge. Man's eternal problems,
including the plight of the poor, can be solved through
a welfare state based on the redistribution of wealth.

— Since we are all children of the globe, subject to
the same rationality, national loyalty and patriotism

are dangerous anachronisms. John Lennon once asked us to "imagine there's no countries": many secularists hope that Lennon's dream will one day blossom into reality.

— The most important goal one can seek is self-transformation, what the psychologist Abraham Maslow called "self-actualization." Maslow intended for this term to describe the fulfillment of one's potential through transcendent "peak experiences." In the present context it refers only to "being all that you can be"-to borrow a phrase from the U.S. military-whether physically, financially, or otherwise.

— Discrimination is the great bugbear of social intercourse. The mandate "judge not, lest ye be judged," stripped of its original meaning as a plea for compassion, is now a justification for closing one's eyes to the difference between right and wrong.

These tenets of secularism will be explored throughout this essay; but for the moment, let us say that, taken together, they form the basis for a seductive new religion. Since this religion is based upon individual, self-directed action as the source of salvation—and upon manifest disapproval of the transcendent—one might just as accurately describe it as a new form of paganism. Unlike Judaism, Christianity, or Islam, secularism does not offer the ethics external to man; its ethics is charted by each man, according to his passions.

There may well be an evangelical revival taking place in America—that "impending theocracy" we hear so much about—but secularism is in its ascendancy, too. Each passing day brings for the secularist new and compelling arguments for "liberation." But secularists, preoccupied with their self-interested quests, overlook the Tocquevillian theme that self-interest is not always well served by focusing on the self.

Secularists also seek to banish religion in ways that go well beyond the religious "intrusion" they decry in public Christmas trees or optional school prayer. Any invocation of God or the ethical principles a legislator believes His existence entails is off-limits in a growing social circle. This is quite ludicrous. Religion remains the font of most Americans' concept of morality, and much legislation is not just a matter of what is most efficacious, but is a choice between two or more different paths, which lawmakers must make using their moral judgment. Insofar as different religions or dogmas result in different visions of morality, a legislator's religion is very much a salient concern.

An immutable morality, handed down from on high, troubles secularists, largely because the refrain of secularism is transformation. Make yourself over, both internally and externally. Secure the symbols of a new life: the car that restores youth, the pills that offer freedom from anxiety, the breezy reads that provide the quick fix of superficial "wisdom." There is no end to the possibilities. Here is the commodification of religion: The "thing" delivers salvation.

When the advocates of secularism claim to be in opposition to religion, they ought to be reminded that, despite protests to the contrary, they speak for and represent a religion of the head and the heart. What they lack is a religion of the soul.

The values embraced by secularists are readily apparent

in the mass media, especially on television shows. Consider the mere premise of "Survivor," the most successful "reality television" program ever. Guile and deceit are rewarded; loyalty and charity are effectively punished. Whoever is most willing to sell out his companions usually wins.

Ronald Reagan noted in his farewell address that culture matters. Indeed it does. That explains why America is presently a bifurcated nation, one where traditional values are sometimes on the defensive, sometimes vigorously embraced.

Secularism has always been at odds with traditional religion, but in the past it was subordinate rather than equivalent. Where these oppositional forces are most vigorously at odds today is in the courts. Prayer in school, sex education, and public religious displays such as nativity scenes and menorahs are hotly contested legal issues. The simplest solution would be for people not to look at such displays if they are offended by them, but this solution doesn't fit the larger secularist agenda to exclude religion from the public square.

The U.S. Supreme Court has held that religion, though not actually prohibited by the Constitution, has virtually no place in public schools—except as an historical narrative. In the 1989 case *Allegheny County v. American Civil Liberties Union*, a nativity scene displayed on the stairs of a county courthouse was ordered removed. The Court held that the display of the nativity scene was unconstitutional because it was displayed by itself. If there had been secular figures such as Santa Claus, reindeer, and snowmen, then the display may have been allowed to stand. This has led to a cultural situation where "holiday songs" have replaced Christmas carols.

Reading assorted elementary-school textbooks, one is tempted to guess that the Pilgrims came to Plymouth Rock for the purpose of sightseeing, not religious freedom. One result of this, maintains James Hitchcock, author of *What Is Secular Humanism*, is that "Americans increasingly grow up religiously illiterate. More importantly, many Americans are uncertain about religious beliefs; and most people find it easier to pursue careers and money than to wrestle with abstract concepts about spiritual enlightenment."

With religion vanishing from America's public square, we can conclude that secularism is on the rise. Whether one notices or not, religion of the soul is in a battle with a religion of personal aggrandizement, which has its own goals, agenda, and view of the future.

2 | Truth as a Relative Concept

"There was a young lady named Bright,
Whose speed was far faster than light,
She set out one day
In a relative way,
And returned home the previous night."
　　　　　— Arthur Henry Reginald Buller, *Limerick*

IS TRUTH RELATIVE? Is it merely a "social construct,"
varying from culture to culture, from context to context?
I've often sat in my ninth-floor university office and challenged those who take this position to exit via the window
instead of the elevators. Not surprisingly, as of this writing,
not one of these relativists has chosen to do so. They know
full well that many of the principles governing human existence are objectively true and apply across the board. The
law of gravity is a dramatic example, and I use it to show that
while some things are open to interpretation, others are
more or less set in stone.

Relativists (whether or not they apply the term to themselves) contend that each person makes his own truth
according to the dictates of conscience. In practice, this more
often means the dictates of convenience, with conscience
always seeming to err on the side of personal benefit. Relativists reject Natural Law, the proposition that certain moral
truths, like scientific ones, are embodied by nature and thus
unchanging, regardless of context. They argue that enduring

religious laws like the Decalogue are of strictly human origin, not only because they are so simplistic but also because they are so unrealistic.

Consider what Christopher Hitchens wrote of the Ten Commandments in his polemic *God is Not Great*: "Instead of the condemnation of evil actions, there is an oddly phrased condemnation of impure thoughts. One can tell that this, too, is a man-made product of the alleged time and place, because it throws in 'wife' along with the other property, animal, human, and material, of the neighbor. More important, it demands the impossible: a recurrent problem with all religious edicts. One may be forcibly restrained from wicked actions, or barred from committing them, but to forbid people from *contemplating* them is too much."

This is a common trope for relativists: If a moral standard is too demanding, if it even sounds too demanding, it should be rejected. But isn't pursuing the impossible a reliable way to ensure that one at least transcends his basest instincts? If instead of submitting to the highest truth everyone becomes architect of his "own" truth, morality is sure to wind up subordinate to the pleasure principle.

In his recent book *Moral Freedom*, Alan Wolfe, a professor of religion and American public life at Boston College, argued that just as the nineteenth century was about economic freedom and the twentieth about political freedom, this century will be about moral freedom. Wolfe believes that we live in an age in which individuals expect to determine for themselves what is right and wrong. He acknowledges that Western thought has long been predicated on the understanding that freedom and moral constraints are complements, not opposites. But he fails to consider the possible negative consequences of a radical departure from this understanding.

Wolfe's hypothesis about the twenty-first century is based on survey research: conversations with Americans from "all walks of life." Unfortunately, his questions are tailored to elicit answers in favor of the new "personal" morality. This may have been a product of Wolfe's inability to see the other side of the coin: Not everybody is willing or able to conjure up his own moral system out of thin air, and many are willing and able to do without morality altogether. Americans are not libertines, according to Wolfe, but they do not generally adhere to traditional concepts of vice and virtue. He contends that "moral freedom" corresponds to a deeply held populist suspicion of authority and a related belief that people know their own best interests. They want to bend rules, but not to be seen as breaking them. Essentially, they inhabit an increasingly complicated world, one which offers countless choices; they want to participate in the definition and interpretation of moral rules.

Though he may believe so, Wolfe's is not a novel way of thinking. Friedrich Nietzsche, too, argued that moral values are neither absolute nor universal. The title of his book *On the Genealogy of Morals* suggests this, in the sense that whatever has a genealogy has come from some earlier iteration of itself. Nietzsche believed that morality is ultimately a function of societal consensus, not of truth. But Nietzsche recognized, at least, that societies do not—cannot—exist without norms, and that, as he saw them, the vast majority of ordinary people follow them. Even when norms are ignored or discarded, new ones inevitably emerge. There can never really be a moral blank slate.

Norms may evolve or change, but they are norms nevertheless. An example: A person exercising his freedom may decide not to recognize a red light as requiring him to stop, and in the absence of coercion, he is free to do so. If enough other people make the same decision and thereby change the norm, the result will be countless accidents, loss of life, and chaos in the streets. And so, individuals mostly bind themselves to the law—enforced or not—especially when living in a society surrounded by other humans, as in the case of the stop light. Norms may change gradually according to the general will, but if people accustom themselves to changing norms *however* and *whenever* they please, *for themselves*, the result would surely be ruination. Just as the threat of collision fosters a norm of traffic safety, so do the dangers of sex—whether life-threatening sexually transmitted diseases or emotional anxiety—inculcate a sense of sexual morality and restraint.

This is why James Q. Wilson has argued that morality is a "natural condition," and why Marc Hauser argues in his recent book *Moral Minds* that "we are born with abstract rules or principles, with nurture entering the picture to set the parameters and guide us toward the acquisition of particular moral systems." Hauser hopes to persuade us that "morality is grounded in biology."

The belief that morality was writ into man's nature has long been a fundamental assumption of most religious moral codes too. "Morality has long been treated as if it were a fixed star," Wolfe observes, and quite rightly. If there is such a thing as human nature—and geneticists are increasingly convinced that there is—something very important is indeed fixed. There have been many iterations of what is called Natural Law. And while it may be right to observe that many Americans today regard the Ten Commandments as ten outdated suggestions, it is surely wrong to suggest that ignoring human nature and social limitations will make the Decalogue's underlying premises go away.

The notion that nothing is fixed, that truth is relative, is itself merely an assumption, one that stands against the intellectual inheritances of philosophy, theology, and biology. In the political sciences, those like Alan Wolfe and the Cato Institute's Brink Lindsey have contended that a lax notion of morality is a natural outgrowth of economic and political freedom. Economic freedom, however, is only healthy when constrained by moral reason, just as political freedom is only effective when the electorate has the educational background to discern the nation's true interests, as Jefferson argued. As a euphemism for the popular divergence from church-bound moralities, "moral freedom" is an oxymoron. Morality is a set of consensual restraints framed by shared and ineffaceable beliefs.

Secularists, with the exception of those postmodernists who openly profess that morality is situational, have long challenged the special role of religion in forging the shared understandings of morality. Christopher Hitchens has often challenged his opponents to "name one ethical statement made, or one ethical action performed, by a believer that could not have been uttered or done by a nonbeliever." Such thinking badly misses the point. The values Hitchens holds in the highest regard—individualism, liberty—have largely been articulated through a Western canon steeped in Christian doctrines like free will and salvation by individual profession. Hitchens's mere claim to secularism does not allow him to escape where and in what tradition he was born: Listen to his pronouncements on matters besides religion, and it becomes clear that he is captive to the West's Judeo-Christian ethics. Had he been born elsewhere in the world, his beliefs would likely look quite different—in no small part thanks to the mark left by religion on any culture.

Really, the burden is on Hitchens and secularists like him to show why moral limitations would exist outside a religion or its intellectual inheritance. This is the flip-side to man's biological inheritance; an animal by his taxonomy, *Homo sapiens* is captive to passions calibrated for his survival. Man may be genetically hard-wired for greater socialization and devotion to his offspring than a typical animal, but the cold hand of evolution also instructs man to do whatever he needs to do to get by and excel. As Dostoevsky wrote, "If God does not exist then everything is permitted."

Where man in his state of nature ends and where a more artificial human society begins is an important philosophical question outside the scope of this essay. But it is no coincidence that philosophers from Aristotle to Kant—and even Camus, a celebrated existentialist—all concluded that morality depends on limits, not freedom. In other words, man needs the added direction and temperance a moral code provides to make his inherent freedom meaningful. Freedom has no value in the absence of norms and constraints. The man who is free to do whatever he wants could easily destroy the freedom of others and annihilate himself. In "The Yellow Bird," a short story by G. K. Chesterton, the protagonist, filled with libertarian zeal, frees his fish from its bowl and watches it die gasping for air. He then liberates his canary from its cage, only to see it eaten by a cat. He then

attempts to liberate his mind from the confines of his brain
—by killing himself. It may be a simple parable, but its message has been surprisingly difficult for many advocates of
moral freedom to grasp on their own.

The teachings of a staid, fixed morality force everyone
who claims to operate within it—the parishioners of a church,
for instance—to position themselves in relation to it. The
rules are unbending and, indeed, often preclude unfailing
compliance: We are all sinners, as Christian churches teach.
But the very term secularism—from the Latin *sæculum*,
meaning "time" or "age"—implies a lack of timelessness and
constancy for the secularists' moral code. As Catholic historian James Hitchcock explains: "To call someone secular
means that he is completely time-bound, totally a child of
his age, a creature of history, with no vision of eternity."
Ethics becomes autonomous and situational, needing no
theological or ideological sanction. Whatever ethical structure well-meaning secularists may devise, their underlying
atheistic creed represents an irreconcilable challenge to a
consistent system of morality, whose existence is not linked
to one man's whims. A secularist's "moral standards," Hitchcock wrote, "tend to be merely those commonly accepted by
the society in which he lives, and he believes that everything
changes, so that there are no enduring or permanent values."
Secularists like Christopher Hitchens benefit because their
moral codes are essentially approximations, though unacknowledged ones, of Judeo-Christian ethics; but if that heritage is left unacknowledged, if Christianity itself continues
to recede, what will secularists take to be their lodestone?

The notion of an inflexible, indeed divinely ordained,
morality has led secularists to present it as the polar opposite

of free will. Typical in this respect was the novelist Isaac Asimov, also a past president of the American Humanists Association, when he claimed that secularists "recognize that it is only when people feel free to think for themselves, using reason as their guide, that they are best capable of developing values that succeed in satisfying human needs and serving human interests." But religion doesn't deny free will; it directs and sustains it. Indeed, there are many religious rites—adult baptism or confirmation, as well as communion—that center on the exercise of parishioners' free will. It is extremely disingenuous to couch one's opposition to faith in the rhetoric of freedom, as though moral choice ceases to exist in the context of religious belief. One's faith may suggest a course of action but it cannot compel it: Only man himself can do that.

Free will may be the bedrock of democratic society, but by itself does not promote the general good. A good society is one in which the citizenry is encouraged to make appropriate decisions constrained by virtue. Russell Kirk wrote in *The Politics of Prudence* that "a society in which men and women are governed by belief in an enduring moral order, by a strong sense of right and wrong, by personal convictions about justice and honor, will be a good society—whatever political machinery it might utilize; while a society in which men and women are morally adrift, ignorant of norms, and intent chiefly upon gratification of appetites, will be a bad society." With its view of transitive morality, secularism leads inexorably to the latter society. It cannot inspire the virtues necessary to sustain a system of active participation, nor does it offer the defenses of moral tradition needed to resist what Abraham Lincoln called "the silent artillery of time."

3 | The Limitations of Science

"The most beautiful thing we can experience is the mysterious. It is the source of all true art and science."
—Albert Einstein, "What I Believe" in *Forum*

IN *Breaking the Spell*, Daniel Dennett argues that evolutionary theory can tell us why human beings are inveterately religious. By showing that we are evolved to believe, Dennett hopes to reduce religious inclinations to a universal human characteristic, no more mysterious than the biological urge to reproduce.

This may seem an astonishing claim, and a sure sign of the hard sciences' ambitions. But secularists have long hoped to erase the premises of serious questions about creation and human nature by limiting "truth" to what science can ascertain. Indeed, science does seek truth. But its purview is limited to the physical world. It can help us to understand how lightning strikes, how plants grow, and why the sky is blue, but it is incapable of answering the major ontological questions: "Where did we come from?" or "Why are we here?" There is a further distinction to be made between science that is objective—verifiable science, that is, in which one observes and tests—and scientism, which proselytizes for the belief that science will ultimately offer explanations that will exhaust the need for a divine creator.

Scientism offers an impossible quest, of course. Verifiable science nearly always generates more questions than it answers; there is every reason to believe that questions about humanity will remain unanswered so long as humans exist. For thousands of years, most people have believed that the world was created by a divine power. Judaism, Christianity, and Islam, in fact all religions, have stories of creation in which God shapes the Earth and mankind. Many people have accepted and drawn strength from the conviction that man was made by God.

But the publication of Charles Darwin's *Origin of Species* in 1859 shook the very foundations of religious faith. Man's faith wasn't shattered by the Theory of Evolution, but it was certainly tested and confused by it. By the close of the twentieth century, many if not most Americans were struggling with how to reconcile their faith and traditions with the scientific revelations encompassed by Darwin's theory. The questions were legion: Is compassion compatible with survival of the fittest? Is self-sacrifice consistent with natural selection?

While Darwin's own account was silent on larger matters of religion, a number of scientists since have waged war against religion using neo-Darwinian accounts of evolution. Stephen Barr, author of *Modern Physics and Ancient Faith*, observes that some scientists have conjured neo-Darwinian hypotheses that subsume all meaningful questions under the banner of scientific inquiry; others, such as Richard Dawkins, contend that complex biological structures arise from unconscious physical processes, thereby negating God and vanquishing teleology. Still others, in the Stephen Jay Gould school of thought, maintain that there is a clear ontological relationship between man and lower animals since we are a product of evolution; we should therefore create an "evolutionary ethics" rather than a religion reliant on natural law. These are examples of scientism, not science.

Whether or not Darwin intended to challenge religious faith, his work has been a rallying cry for those who would like to undercut religion's reason for being. It was the dream of Darwin's disciples to have every truth explicitly and precisely stated, and to formulate every step in the chain of logical deductions until a "theory of everything" emerged. Scientific history is littered with examples of those who have sought a complete system of knowledge. Nonetheless, when Kurt Gödel wrote his *Incompleteness Theorem* in the early twentieth century, these illusions were shattered. Gödel proved that a logical system of propositions cannot be both complete and true. If a system is complete (or, as logicians say, closed) some truths will fall outside of it.

Instead of speaking of scientific knowledge, it is probably more realistic, in my judgment, to speak of what Werner Heisenberg called "indeterminacy." After all, science is the process of knowing, of rethinking, redrawing and reconceptualizing. If science were to remain static, it simply wouldn't be science any longer.

The world that views truth solely as the province of science must also content itself with the proposition that morals are purely man's creation, uninspired by providential will. Bertrand Russell recognized the implications of this position, and argued that, "What the world needs is not dogma but an attitude of scientific inquiry combined with a belief that the torture of millions is not desirable, whether inflicted by Stalin or by a Deity imagined in the likeness of the believer." While Russell discredits religion and its dogmas, boy knows. Yet just as frequently, traditional religions have existed in harmony with science and have even helped it along. Some of history's greatest scientists have been devout Christians, a fact which should give pause to those who think of science and faith as irreconcilable. Kepler, Pascal, Boyle, and Descartes were all strong believers. Sir Isaac Newton wrote extensively on the subject of Christian theology. Presumably it raised questions and provided answers with which science did not and could not concern itself.

Just as prayer is not a substitute for thinking, neither is rational exegesis a complete explanation for physical phenomena, much less for moral or ontological phenomena. Even scientific postulations that probe deepest into creation and prescribe physical causes to the very origins of the universe leave open an ontological question of who, so to speak, lit the fuse. Indeed, the Vatican Observatory—one of the world's renowned astronomical research centers—has long held the church's understanding of Genesis, *creatio ex nihilo*, to be consistent with the Big Bang theory.

The sociologist Rodney Stark from Baylor University argues in his work *Victory of Reason*, "there is no inherent conflict between religion and science," and claims that "Christian theology was essential for the rise of science." As an organized discipline, science arose first and foremost under the auspices of religious orders. If Christianity had wanted to squelch science and rational thought, it could have done so. Yet science flourished in countries that embraced Christianity as their official state religion. This was no accommodation, no arrangement of convenience. Theology and science share the same spirit of inquiry, though they approach inquiry from different angles, and the two were and remain for the most part perfectly capable of working in tandem toward knowledge.

Too many clerics and scientists alike envision a false dichotomy between faith and science today, even though men of faith married reason to religion for centuries. Medieval Christianity, Stark notes, depicted God "as a rational, responsive, dependable, and omnipotent being, and the universe as his personal creation. The natural world was thus understood to have a rational, lawful, stable structure, awaiting (indeed, inviting) human comprehension." Christians could not have contemplated God without having faith in reason as a tool of understanding. Arguably the most important theological work ever written, Thomas Aquinas's *Summa Theologica*, is fundamentally a grandiose effort (3,000 pages in all) to relate a heavenly God to the material world. Reason, moreover, remains a powerful tool of Christian theology today. Pope Benedict's lecture at Regensburg University was, in fact, an exploration of faith's basis in reason. (Early in his lecture, he sought to explain "why spreading the faith through violence is something unreasonable," and in doing so set off a reaction in the Muslim world that eclipsed the actual message of his speech).

Universities, of course, sprang up throughout Europe as organs of the Christian Church. Theology was the primary subject in early universities, but this was soon supplemented with courses in mathematics and the natural sciences. Christians were eager to understand the world that God had created for them. Roger Bacon, a Franciscan priest who taught at Oxford University in the thirteenth century, expressed Christian faith in scientific inquiry. He wrote, "Without experiment, nothing can be adequately known.

An argument proves theoretically, but does not give the certitude necessary to remove all doubt; nor will the mind repose in the clear view of truth, unless it finds it by way of experiment." Scientific experiments were common at Oxford University in the 1200s. Robert Grosseteste, one of the chancellors of Oxford University at that time, is widely considered to be one of the first men to clearly formulate the necessary steps for carrying out a scientific experiment. Even in its early years, Oxford University showed that probing scientific research and Christian religious beliefs could exist and flourish in close contact with one another.

In the 1990s, a survey of American scientists indicated that about forty percent of them believe in God and life after death. This figure should persuade us that traditional religious beliefs and science are still compatible, despite tellingly enthusiastic claims to the contrary. Some scientists have even embraced the concept of "intelligent design." As its numerous critics have pointed out, intelligent design is not, strictly speaking, a "theory": It does not provide a testable hypothesis about the origins of the universe. Instead, we might call it an acknowledgment of the many facets of existence that science cannot adequately explain. Those who promote "intelligent design" are interested primarily in assuring us that there is not yet any reason to discard the "creator." Science has explained a great deal, but it has done more to remind us of our ever-humbling ignorance.

The secularist belief that science can fully interpret human experience is, conversely, a belief that time spent studying traditional religions and theology is time wasted. In his *God Is Not Great*, Christopher Hitchens repeatedly exhorts his readers to look at the Hubble telescope's photographs—

photographs, he maintains, of things far more awe-inspiring and instructive than the works of theologians. Not for him the peaceful coexistence of spiritual and scientific awe. There is only what is available to our senses and our reason, nothing more.

Werner Heisenberg wrote that "we cannot disregard the fact that science is formed by men. Natural science does not simply describe and explain nature, it is part of the interplay between nature and ourselves; it describes nature as exposed to our method of questioning. This was a possibility of which Descartes could not have thought but it makes sharp separation between the world and the I impossible." The limits of the human mind have been expressed in the work of the mathematician and philosopher Gottfried von Leibniz who differentiated knowledge obtainable through reason and observation and knowledge emanating from the soul. He did not see religion as incompatible with reason; he held, in fact, that God was present in everything in the world, even in sensory knowledge.

It is indeed doubtful that scientists will ever be able to fully explain the universe. Secularists base their belief in the power of science primarily on faith, a faith in what *might* be uncovered in the future. The expression "having faith in science" may sound strange. Scientists rely on concrete proof for their "code of beliefs"; once scientists give sufficient proof for a hypothesis, it is accepted. Nevertheless, as the historian Daniel J. Boorstin noted, "The greatest obstacle to discovery is not ignorance—it is the illusion of knowledge." Secularists, armed with science, are guilty of thinking that they know more than they actually do.

"Society in every state is a blessing, but Government, even in its best state, is but a necessary evil, in its worst state, an intolerable one."
— Thomas Paine, *Common Sense*

THE DOGMA THAT science can prescribe solutions to all of humanity's problems and ontological questions has a pernicious corollary.

One can see it in the official approval political and intellectual leaders of the early twentieth century lavished on eugenics, the vain and dangerous belief that man could purge and magnify certain inheritable genetic traits for the "betterment of mankind." And one can see it still today, at those points where the state has free rein to engage in wealth redistribution to attempt to level the economy, or to act as watchman for economic progress through the power of eminent domain. Once science is seen as a force of inquiry capable of answering all questions, it is a small leap to believing that government can put those answers into practice and solve humanity's enduring problems.

There is plenty of evidence from historians and economists alike that high taxes, wealth redistribution, and government intervention are not the path to utopia. Yet even in the twenty-first century, secularists refuse to be disabused of the idea that sweeping, "progressive" strategies can improve the lot of mankind. One wonders what will be the next heartbreaking illustration of the fact that, as Russell Kirk once simply and firmly rendered it, "Economic leveling . . . is not economic progress."

The secularist faith in human institutions leads to a mistaken conviction that the government is a more competent and just distributor than the "invisible hand" of the free market. This is also a basic principle of socialist governments. Ironically, given their assumption that mankind is the only repository of wisdom and grace, secularists have little faith in the individual to determine the scope and breadth of his wealth. Income *disparity* is what offends them.

One sees this in domestic policy, with calls to reduce the pay of corporate executives, and in international comparisons between the haves and have-nots. In Democratic politics, it has become axiomatic that the rich grow richer while the poor grow poorer. Those who demonstrate against the World Trade Organization are on the whole skeptical, rather than welcoming, of economic growth, thinking that it takes place at the expense of the world's poorest.

A study by David Dollar and Aart Kraay of the World Bank presents a very different reality. Over four decades, the researchers sampled growth and income in eighty countries, and found that growth raises income for the poor on a one-to-one ratio with the rise in incomes overall. In other words, free trade spurs growth to a significant degree—with the poor participating fully in its rewards—notwithstanding anti-globalist claims to the contrary.

Dollar and Kraay not only found that reducing public spending and inflation promotes growth, but also that cutting the size of government has a salutary influence on the condition of the poor. On a superficial level, this finding is surprising, since so much of public spending is designed to assist the poor. But as the U.S. "War on Poverty" has demonstrated during its decades-long existence, the largest beneficiaries of such programs are often middle-class bureaucrats.

Surely this thoughtful study should challenge the suppositions of the growing throng of protectionists worldwide. But, sadly, it has barely disturbed them, much less shaken their foundations. This is so because even a one-for-one income improvement between rich and poor doesn't alter their relative economic standing. Even when growth disproportionately benefits the poor, one can still claim the rich grow richer and poor, poorer: Suppose a person earning $10,000 somewhere in the Third World improves his income by 10 percent while someone earning $1,000 improves his income by 50 percent. Although the poor person enjoys a faster rate of growth, the income spread between the two parties will nonetheless widen from $9,000 to $9,500. This perspective is one that invariably insinuates itself into U.N. statistical profiles to justify additional Western aid.

By definition, a stratified society will have rich people, poor people, and people in between. And history has taught us that even a government-contrived "equality" merely fosters the exaggeration of marginal income differences. Such was the case in the days of the Soviet Union, where the size of one's apartment and rations allotment were objects of envy; indeed, one enduring legacy of Soviet "equality" is that Russian culture remains obsessed with such comparisons.

The Dollar-Kraay study suggests, as others have sagely done, that introducing and enforcing the rule of law, protecting private property, and encouraging openness and free trade are the essential components of a national policy that wishes both to generate wealth and alleviate poverty in absolute, not relative, terms.

Those who believe in the power of free markets are not surprised by Dollar and Kraay's conclusion. But it still does not address the nagging complaint that class stratification in the United States is widening. The rehearsal of this theme in the media is rarely challenged; it is an idea elevated to the pantheon of untouchable subjects, "facts" that "everybody knows" but few are ever called upon to prove.

In fact, the richest one percent of U.S. households owned approximately 35 percent of total wealth not just in 2003, but in 1933, 1953, 1983, and 1993. That ratio may sadden those of us who aren't in that top one percent, or upset those who entertain radically egalitarian notions and inveigh against an American oligarchy. But it is worth asking whether the top one percent is even made up of the same families from one generation to the next. As it happens, the movement into and out of this elite is quite substantial. Because of the tendency of even a large, inflation-adjusted reserve of money to seem much less large after decades of economic growth, there is little or nothing to guarantee alpha status between generations.

Hysterical claims about widening income inequality have their purpose, most of all as rhetorical appeals to win unthinking approval for a "soak the rich" tax. And, indeed, while the percentage of their total holdings has not changed, the wealthiest one percent has picked up more and more of the tab for government spending. The top one percent paid about 20 percent of all tax revenue in 1983, about 22 percent in 1993, and about 34 percent in 2004. Americans at the upper end of the income scale are seeing their portion of the federal income tax burden steadily increase.

What escapes mention in discussion of tax policies is that there isn't any difference between a tax of zero and a tax of 100 percent. A zero-percent tax derives no revenue for the government, and a 100-percent tax rate constitutes an absolute disincentive to work—and consequently yields zero revenue for the government. The essence of contemporary capitalism is to find taxation's middle ground, which can at once provide for budgetary essentials while not imposing needless disincentives on labor.

Populist declarations and tax hikes seem to make so little practical difference not only because of the government's general inefficiency, but because, past their tipping point, people will reduce their effort and tax revenues will drop off. On this point, we return to the delusive notion of Karl Marx, who inspired socialist goals by declaring a just system of human society to take "from each according to his ability, [and give] to each according to his need." Here was a position that seemingly embraced fairness instead of exploitation. But such thinking defies common sense and human experience. Why should people apply their ability in order to satisfy the needs of others? What incentives exist, absent self-interest, for people to apply their ability? It is an old joke, but a perceptive one, that in socialist nations people don't work hard and are paid accordingly.

The freedom to express one's ability yields financial rewards to the individual proportionate to his ability. This differential reward system offends radical egalitarians, but it is part and parcel of the incentives that lubricate the economy—and ultimately provide for human welfare. Sustained government spending, as well as private charity, depends on the generation of wealth.

Those states that erect as few barriers as possible to the production of wealth are where innovation and resourcefulness take hold. It is no surprise that those Western countries that have folded scientific and technological development into organs of the state—a tack for which France, with its many national commissions, is justifiably infamous—have seen very little home-grown ingenuity in the fastest-moving industries of the day.

Many criteria distinguish growing economies from stagnant ones. But the presence of a dynamic civil society is an essential trait of prosperous states. In this condition, it is recognized that individual human action is the decisive factor in society—"*man, himself,* that is, his knowledge," in the words of Pope John Paul II. The spirit of collectivization is an encumbrance, not an ally, to real progress. It is for this reason that any state that wishes to enter the ranks of high-octane world economies must first recognize individual liberties, private property, and the rule of law as the prerequisites from which other considerations issue and evolve.

There is no clearer demonstration of the necessity of these building blocks than in their absence. In the so-called Third World, the power wielded by the state and its politicians has led to a situation where private property and other individual rights can easily be trammeled or, in any case, are never fully secured.

Wealth generation is not a mystical process reliant on political alchemy. It is the culmination of intentional structuring, habits built into a nation's fabric. The great advantage that the United States has on the world stage is not merely its capital accumulation, nor its abundance of technically proficient entrepreneurs. Rather, it is the Constitution, law, and public spirit that have ensured a free and open society. The pursuit of private property—which social-contract philosopher John Locke deemed the driving force of human political society—has been a cornerstone of American life since the eighteenth century. Compared with other Western states, entrepreneurship is encouraged, and public ownership is limited. In Germany, for instance, the declaration of bankruptcy precludes board membership in a public company. In the United States, by contrast, bankruptcy is a sign of trial and error, risk-taking, and presumably one's having learned appropriate lessons. Almost every successful entrepreneur in Silicon Valley has, at one point in his professional life, filed for bankruptcy.

Against the argument that laws and institutions matte generations of optimists have imagined that unfree so eties naturally tend toward freedom—such was said of Soviet Union for decades, the same thing is said of Chi today. There is frighteningly little empirical evidenc support this conclusion, and simply to assume as much ignore an historical and human propensity to accum power and impose one's own will on a population.

Out of this fallacy emerges another that Americans do well to pay heed: that free societies will, by inertia, rem free. It is hard, indeed, to abolish freedoms in democracy, with everyone (so the conventional wisdom goes) watching and participating. But it is not as hard as one thinks.

It is easy to miss the gradual erosion of Americans' property rights. How many people, for instance, could call upon their recollections or intuitions for data on socioeconomic groups' varying tax burdens? One's paycheck, as much as one's land, is "property"—and by any absolute standard, taxpayers are paying much, much more to the government each decade, without any concomitant, increased responsibility of government to fund basic needs, whether infrastructure or public education.

Taxation, if not undertaken for legitimate causes of government, already offends the right to property. But there is no more obvious manifestation of the government's encroachment on the individual's right to property than the recent expansion of the use of eminent domain, as the power of the government to seize private property is known.

Once, eminent domain was an uninhibited indulgence of government. In the employ of the exiled English royal court, Hobbes argued that since a sovereign king held ultimate ownership over all land in his realm, an individual could not refuse a sale to the sovereign as he could rebuff an ordinary citizen. Republicanism, however, did not countenance such an unbounded power. The U.S. Constitution's Fifth Amendment curtailed the monarchical right, `··· ··` distinct conditions on the exercise of eminent doma.. taking of private property had to be made in the interest of "public use" and "just compensation" had to be paid to its owner.

Gradually, that right has been eroded, most recently in the 2005 Supreme Court case *Kelo v. City of New London*. Here, the owners of fifteen homes in the Fort Trumbull neighborhood of New London, Connecticut—including one woman who was born in her house eighty-seven years prior and had lived there ever since—had their property appropriated by the New London municipal government, which argued that "public use" trumped the protection of private property. In court, the city argued that the parastatal New London Development Corporation had a right to take the homes because it planned to build an economic center that would benefit the entire community. Revenue from the taxes would help the town, the planners claimed, and employment would climb.

Justice John Paul Stevens, part of the Court majority, cited past allowances of eminent domain in helping a gold-mining company in the redistribution of land ownership in Hawaii, and in the redevelopment of a neighborhood in Washington, D.C. If this was "public use" under the Constitution, why wouldn't New London's economic center qualify; after all, as Stevens wrote, "The city [New London] has carefully formulated a development plan."

Justice Sandra Day O'Connor countered this tendentious argument: "Under the banner of economic development, all private property is now vulnerable to being taken and transferred to another private owner, so long as it might be upgraded. . . . The specter of condemnation hangs over all property. Nothing is to prevent the state from replacing any Motel 6 with a Ritz-Carlton, any home with a shopping mall, or any farm with a factory." Justice O'Connor concluded that "the government now has license to transfer property from those with fewer resources to those with more. The Founders cannot have intended this perverse result."

There is more than a whiff of Orwellian illogic to the Court majority's decision. Kelo is as good a reminder as any that a government—or in the case of the federal American model, the national, state, and municipal *governments*—can just as easily take away a right as vouchsafe it. In government's social programming, a utilitarian standard has been applied to property through eminent domain, where the rights of the few are trampled in order to promote the supposed economic benefits of the many.

What ails us is ultimately the ambition of the government. Why hasn't government learned the lessons of history, that class stratification is a function of a free market; that illegitimacy and resulting poverty are often caused by forms of social pathology; that aging and health problems are the inescapable punishments of Father Time? These problems have plagued society from its very beginnings, and as often as government has tried to tackle them, government has failed. Even so, it is difficult for secular humanists to concede that some matters are beyond government control. I turn now to evaluate where and why government has failed.

5 | Patriotism as a Moral Problem

"What do we mean by patriotism in the context of
our times? ... A patriotism that puts country ahead
of self; a patriotism which is not short, frenzied out-
bursts of emotion, but the tranquil and steady dedication of a lifetime."
— Adlai Stevenson, Speech New York City 1952

WE HAVE SEEN in previous chapters how religion wed-
ded society to a common system of ethics, and how religion
and science served as partners in inquiry. Religion and civil
society were also once inseparable. Organized religion provided the education, the health care, and the other forms of
social welfare that are today, almost without exception, the
province of governments.

In the twentieth century, secularists were foremost
among those who pinned their hopes on the state to sup-
plant the church in its historic role. But the major secular
ideologies failed to offer a replacement for the galvanizing
effect religion worked on the public spirit. Nationalism
proved an ideology without universal appeal, prone to violence when it collided with the equally fervent (and equally
exclusive) nationalism of a neighboring state. And social-
ism's doctrine of "from each according to his abilities, to
each according to his needs" failed to instill mass altruism.
Government, it seemed, could not command the moral loy-
alties of the populace in the same way that religion could.

The Right and the Left can today agree that American

civil society is eroding. When polled, most Americans believe that their society has become atomized and impersonal. Robert D. Putnam describes the decreasing adherence to voluntary organizations and community activities as the "bowling alone" phenomenon.

There can be little doubt that part of the blame for this must fall on secularism. Today's secularists celebrate the mental freedom from church-bound religious ethics that Thomas Paine imagined, in tandem with a drive for individual self-fulfillment (which often merely amounts to self-pleasure). This attitude surely has played a large role in subordinating community spirit to radical individualism.

A lack of private, individual devotion to the welfare of one's community, of course, has not meant that governments are incapable of creating public-welfare entitlements— indeed, they summon programs and agencies into being at a rate like never before. But the rise of the bureaucratic state has been the occasion of what Harvard sociologist Daniel Bell has called a loss of *civitas*, that "spontaneous willingness to obey the law, to respect the rights of others, to forgo enrichment at the expense of the public weal."

Civitas, by another name, is patriotism: a selfless devotion to one's society and the citizens who constitute it. This respect for law and community had its roots in religion Alexis de Tocqueville observed during his famous visit to America in the 1830s. He wrote in *Democracy in America*: "I sought for the key to the greatness and genius of America in her harbors . . . in her fertile fields and boundless forests; in her rich mines and vast world commerce; in her public school system and institutions of learning. I sought for it in her democratic Congress and in her matchless Constitution. Not until I went into the churches of America and heard her pulpits flame with righteousness did I understand the secret of her genius and power." Today, nearly two centuries on, it is no coincidence that the most generous donors to charities are religious Americans, particularly those who identify themselves as doctrinally conservative, like evangelical Protestants.

Without a transcendent force to guide and shape one's life, many forms of self-indulgence emerge and take over. Americans have lurched into the "age of me." Many expect fame simply for "being themselves," and self-esteem divorced from any compelling reason for it has become an important goal from nursery school on up to adulthood. Americans are preoccupied with advertisements for themselves. This is evident in inflated resumes, talk radio blustering, cocktail party conversation, and post-game banter. To paraphrase a saying from Lake Wobegon, everyone is the greatest—just ask them.

For secularists, individual aspiration is the hallmark of the "good life." Abraham Maslow's concept of "self-actualization" has been raised by popular culture to a matter of almost transcendent importance. I say "almost" because there can be nothing genuinely transcendent about self-love at the expense of humility and concern for others. The Greeks, observing the phenomenon, called it hubris. In the Book of Proverbs it is memorably condemned by the saying "Pride goeth before a fall."

Money, self-aggrandizement, celebrity status, and power are the contemporary versions of the Golden Calf. They are pursued with religious fervor, but when obtained, they rarely satisfy the recipient in the manner anticipated. But the race goes on, and the emptiness grows, a function of a spiritual void in an overrated quest for attention. Biblical prophets warned that one must walk humbly in the face of God; contemporary media prophets contend that showing off is its own reward.

Those who exist under the presumption that they are the best are setting themselves up for a fall. One may well ask: Why should hubris *inevitably* lead to a fall from grace? What is there about hubristic behavior that brings about opprobrium and failure?

Ian Fleming, the creator of James Bond, provides an answer: His villains exhibit monstrous vanity. Various Bond nemeses claim, almost comically, "I am invincible" or "I cannot be stopped" or "The world will be mine." It is in these declarations that a weakness is found, the weakness that the MI5 agent exploits. A belief in invincibility sets in motion circular thinking: I cannot be defeated; hence I need not concern myself with potential rivals.

From the Maginot Line to the Roman Empire, history has been colored by this pernicious delusion. In fact, an empire is often most at risk at its greatest heights. British dominance of the world's sea lanes in the nineteenth century did not countenance a rival, much less one with access to the Baltic. Yet Germany developed a navy at the very moment the British stopped investing in what was regarded as the world's leading naval force. British leaders could not contemplate a genuine adversary in the seas they ruled.

Nor does humility find a happy home in American politics. The administration of Lyndon Johnson was predicated on the hubristic notion that, given sufficient political support and adequate resources, it could eradicate perennial social problems. Despite the expenditure of trillions of dollars since the 1960s, the problems persist, as does an exaggerated confidence in the power of technocrats who in many cases have not themselves digested the lessons of history.

This over-confidence is a bipartisan affliction. In 1992, the recently elected President Bill Clinton said that his would be "the most ethical administration in American history"—a boast that requires no comment. But Newt Gingrich did no better, doing everything possible to feed the illusion that he possessed political ingenuity others did not after engineering the 1994 Republican victory. His hubristic sentiments set a low bar for his political opponents to attack him. Every minor gaffe was put under the microscope of journalism until this Republican king of the hill lost his position and his power. Intelligence without humility is a prescription for failure.

If politicians are not exemplars for the average American, neither are those who move in the world of Big Business. An archetype of the 1980s corporate raider, Saul Steinberg launched assaults on Disney and Chemical Bank, and became a billionaire (the richest self-made American under 30, according to *Forbes*). He and his wife were on every "A-list" in town. The Steinbergs "were very much a part of that whole ostentatious wealth era," says Ken Auletta, a critic of corporate America. "You have it, you flaunt it, you show it off." Yes—and then you lose it. Steinberg's drop back to earth was as precipitous as his rise. By 2001, his Reliance Insurance Group, built as the launch pad for audacious corporate raids, had been forced into liquidation itself. The fall was unsurprising. Once Steinberg boasted "I'll own the world" and "I could even be the first Jewish President," his fate was sealed. An obsession with the acquisition of material things, one dimension of the secularist creed, often if not always results in despair.

It is telling that so many of the companies that have bought the rights to name stadiums have fallen into financial difficulty or bankruptcy—Enron, T.W.A., PSI Net, Fruit of the Loom, 3 Com, Conseco, CMGI Inc., the list goes on and on. A belief in invincibility is hubris's handmaiden, and leads to complacency and ruin. The GM building in midtown Manhattan, the IBM tower, the AT&T edifice, and the E. F. Hutton building have become monuments to an empty corporate largesse.

Irrational exuberance for oneself is not delimited by Wall Street or the Beltway, however. It has seeped into mass culture as well. Once held to be heroes for their sportsmanship and humility, professional athletes have come to embody hubris.

In this regard, the World Basketball Championship is an instructive event. In 2002, when it was held in Indianapolis, the U.S. team comprised five NBA players, some of them All Stars. But as Coach George Karl later admitted, the team simply assumed that its athletic skill was sufficient to ensure a championship win. The players on the court performed as five individuals, but never as a team. They dribbled between their legs, settled for three-point shots, and simply neglected to play defense. In the second round, the U.S. lost to Argentina 87–80, despite the impression that the U.S. team was far more talented than its rival. It lost to Yugoslavia in another game. And in its final match, the U.S. lost once more —to Spain, a team without a single NBA player. This was a rout beyond any previously endured by an American team.

When selected for the 2006 American team, Elton Brand

said of the 2002 tournament, "We must guard against cockiness." Yet in his year, U.S. players warmed up by putting on a "jam session" for the fans. One player after another dunked emphatically as the crowd roared its appreciation. At the other end of the floor Greece—like Spain, a team without a single NBA player—quietly shot free throws. The U.S. team, with all its dazzling skill on display, lost to the Greeks 101–95.

Staying humble is hard, especially in a largely secular society. An athlete, businessman, or politician was once seen as one part of a larger social order, and expected to behave as such. But personal fulfillment, where self trumps self-restraint or self-sacrifice, exerts a morally crippling influence.

This cult of the self is, at its core, inimical to *civitas*—patriotism. Properly understood, patriotism demands self-sacrifice and rejects the modern creed of self-fulfillment. A patriot's loyalty is more emotional, and less apparently rational. The epistemology of the religious mind—one that has a place for both reason and passion—no doubt provides greater room than the skeptic's mind for patriotism to take hold.

Secularists recoil both at the communal outlook of patriotism, and at what they regard as a perverse emotional entanglement between citizen and state—to them, it smacks of religiosity. But in an important way, patriotism is an emotional value that has its roots in pragmatism. As genetics' cold rationale wires a parent to show highly emotional preference for one's own offspring, the patriotic citizen is drawn to his community and state. Genetics forges an emotional bond because, in the long run, prosperous children make for secure parents; and Locke, Hobbes, and the other major social contractors would be among those to note that *civitas*'s or patriotism's practical benefit is self-preservation.

To the faithful, patriotism can be a force to gird a country against seemingly insurmountable hardship. But to the skeptic, "patriotism" evokes a nation behaving irrationally— rallying around the flag, regardless of right or wrong. Indeed, the belief that patriotism is a simplistic and outmoded attitude has some merit. National pride has played a role in the outbreak of many wars. Prior to World War II, Japan and Germany both believed fervently in their own superiority. Feeling invulnerable and divinely ordained, Japan went to war with many Asian nations before attacking the United States at Pearl Harbor. Similarly, Germany went on a crusade to conquer Europe and very nearly did. But if blind nationalism played a dangerous role in Germany and Japan during WWII, American (and British) national pride surely had a positive effect. It is doubtful that citizens of Allied countries would have tolerated food rationing, mass conscription, and shortages in raw materials without a sense that their country stood for something fundamentally good, that it was *in the right*.

In the United States armed forces, the importance of patriotism is easiest to see in its absence. During the Vietnam War, many American citizens turned against the war and protested, resisted the draft, and otherwise disrupted the war effort. Soldiers were frequently demoralized. Patriotism itself came into question. While the North Vietnamese could not defeat the United States on the battlefield, they could undermine American confidence and win the war in the corridors of Congress. This is a point that has not been lost on the terrorists intent on forcing U.S. forces out of Iraq.

Patriotism is a powerful sentiment, but an often indispensable one. It is essential to draw the line between a patriotic belief in the good of a country's principles and actions in defense of them, and a nationalist love of one's nation regardless of the circumstances.

Today, simple acts of well-meaning patriotism—the very kind that remind Americans of their laudable national ideals —are subject to ridicule. It was altogether typical when, after 9/11, a popular comedian asked, to the enthusiastic approval of his audience, "Has that flag-waving, cheerleading, rah-rah bullshit stopped or died down at all?" When patriotism no longer captivates, people resist the symbols of the state, regarding them as false, cloying, and manipulative.

The Pledge of Allegiance, which simply articulates America's commitment to liberty, goes unrecited at most public events; likewise, the Star-Spangled Banner is usually left unsung. Both the pledge and anthem are compositions with a religious tone, and secularists regard anything beyond their perfunctory usage to be evidence of parochial attitudes. Forthrightly patriotic people, those quaint enough to believe these national mantras hold some truth, are increasingly seen as "rednecks."

Today, in American mass culture, one sees a more subtle decoupling of America from the values it was once seen to comprise. Once Superman's motto was, "Truth, justice, and the American way"; now, the screenwriters of *Superman Returns* have rewritten it as, "Truth, justice, and all that stuff." It spells trouble when so quintessentially American a figure as Superman becomes a harbinger of self-doubt.

At least Superman is a mass-culture icon who stands up for the public good—this is not always so. Today, attention or recognition is the main standard by which public icons are judged, and any act that draws newsprint or television space, however questionable, becomes acceptable. As one press agent put it, "Nothing can propel a career like scandal." Current journalistic practice seems to appeal to the superficial and banal. Here today, gone tomorrow. It's as if Andy Warhol were selecting the personalities now routinely profiled on the front pages of formerly serious newspapers.

The hotel heiress Paris Hilton became a celebrity after a series of well-publicized sexual peccadilloes. The actress Lindsay Lohan receives attention for alcoholic binges and temper tantrums. These are people who, as Daniel Boorstin noted, are fully engaged in *being* celebrities. As Paris Hilton explained her own role, "There is no one in the world like me. I think every decade has an iconic blonde—like Marilyn Monroe or Princess Diana—and right now, I'm that icon." This is an unvarnished peek into the mind of manufactured celebrity. It does not require discernible talent or capacity for public service. Celebrities are, to use a popular phrase, famous for being famous.

As the standards of public approbation have vanished like soap bubbles, only recognition counts. Never mind that Madonna's marketing takes the form of public nudity, blasphemy, depicting herself in degrading sexual acts, and the rest of her unique brand of immorality. She is, as they say in the business, recognizable, and that means easy to sell. Marketing undergirds the manufacture of celebrity, and getting people to notice you is all that counts, so handlers push the envelope of attention, forcing the culture to new extremes. What was avant-garde yesterday is passé today. Recently a young man who committed a savage murder said, unrepentantly, "Well, at least now I'll be noticed." Alas, he was correct.

Infamy and *fame* had distinct meanings some time ago. *Infamy* designated a reputation derived from evil, brutal, and criminal acts; and *fame* stemmed from doing something positive and valuable. Tupac Shakur was infamous, not famous. Paris Hilton is infamous, not famous. It may be in the interest of *National Enquirer* or *Star* to confuse these words, but to those who realize that civilization rests on a gossamer-thin foundation of norms and traditions, it is clear that such tears at the fabric of society are not easily repaired. Fame and infamy must be disentangled. When people derive celebrity from acts of genuine charity, concern for others, and behavior that should be emulated, we should call them famous—and only then.

When our mass culture forsakes the expectation that those in public life are moral exemplars, it is little surprise that a nation cannot be imagined to be on a moral mission. NYU historian Thomas Bender criticizes the very notion of national identity in his new book, *A Nation Among Nations: America's Place In World History*. In Bender's words, national histories "are taught in schools and brought into public discourses to forge and sustain national identities, presenting the self-contained nation as the natural carrier of history. That way of writing and teaching history has exhausted itself." Bender is not alone in this conviction: A creeping transnationalism has taken the place of the belief that a nation can be a champion for good. Amy Guttman, president of the University of Pennsylvania, and Richard Sennett, a sociologist and distinguished scholar at NYU, both share this transnational bias. There is a point to be made, albeit an obvious one: The history of one nation is related to events in other nations. That point aside, there are a number of questions the transnationalists must confront. What does it mean to be a citizen of the globe? How can the glaring difference in national character between, say, the United States and Saudi Arabia be reconciled to a universal transnationalism? Are there not exceptional characteristics in American history that should be emphasized?

To John Stuart Mill, national identity established "a *prima facie* case for uniting all the members of [that] nationality under the same government, and a government to themselves apart." Mill made a reasonable assumption, one as true today as in his time—that different peoples would give rise to separate states with different national characters. Transnationalism discards this logic, or at least refuses to heed its implication that a national character is easier to wield for good than erase entirely. The alternative—an unreasonable one that "post-national" historians and theorists have posited—is to be like Kant's imaginary "citizen of the world," given form by all the diverse proclivities of the "community of nations."

This conceptual equality of nations is written in stone at the United Nations, where its internal contradictions are on full display. Consider the U.N. Commission on Human Rights, now called the Human Rights Council, where a bid to limit membership to only those states who respect human rights on their turf was rejected, paradoxically, with the claim that all people have a stake in human rights. Indeed, all people do have a stake, but to imagine that Sudan's people (or anyone else) were meaningfully represented by the seat that government had on the commission in 2005 is fanciful in the extreme. The very notion of human rights is necessarily devalued in a body that does not differentiate between tyrannies and democracies. Faith put in the U.N.—the closest thing to the imaginary "community of nations"—is surely more naïve than patriotic faith in many a country.

Ultimately, it is the differences between governments that count. To be a patriot is not to think one's country is flawless, but to believe that it is capable of doing good, if only by relative comparison to a neighbor. The patriot imagines a nation, observes a state, and works to reconcile the two. There can be little question that the United States' national character is exceptional, having been a harbinger for human liberty and equality; and, too, in practice, America's history is a narrative of one of the *most* open, prosperous, and free societies the world has known.

Americans need to reappropriate the pride they once held for their country. That is a difficult calling at a time when secularism deprecates the heartfelt nature of patriotism. Patriotism requires a fuller measure of devotion that the mere fixtures of government can command: It is not enough to believe in a state and its many organs; one must believe in the state's nature and its mission. This was a patriotic passion facilitated, as has been noted, by popular religion and mass culture in the early days of the American republic. And just as Tocqueville thought that religious fervor in service of national values was a force that could make America great, he also warned against the soft despotism of state authority. The bureaucracy of the state can, and has, supplanted civil society's role in carrying out a perceived national mission.

Civil society's gradual erosion has prompted some efforts to save it from further self-destruction. Early in his administration, President Bush announced an initiative to enlist private (and typically parochial) charity organizations in social-welfare projects—an attempt to embolden feelings of individual and community duty to the public welfare. It is unlikely that the measure can succeed in the current political climate, but the reemergence of this Tocquevillian strategy is certainly unexpected and intriguing.

"When the religion of a people is destroyed," Tocqueville argued, "doubt gets hold of the highest portions of the intellect, and half paralyses all the rest of its powers." From Toynbee to Sorokin and from Tyler to Spengler, historians have confronted civilizations that lose their will to survive, lose their confidence in their political organization, or become purely pleasure-seeking entities. Tyler even charted a trajectory common to the world's greatest civilizations, which arcs "from bondage to spiritual faith; from spiritual faith to great courage; from courage to liberty; from liberty to abundance; from abundance to complacency; from complacency to apathy; from apathy to dependence; from dependence back into bondage."

The parallels to our own democracy are evident. It is foolish to expect enduring national success absent the community-minded patriotism needed to sustain it. But this is precisely the recipe proposed by America's cult of the self, in its hubris, in its mindless glamour, and in its unwillingness to defend the very values of liberty and openness that give self-obsession preening room. Ours is a dangerous complacency. To overcome it, we need something on the lines of the religion Tocqueville saw in the up-and-coming republic: a belief in and a sense of national purpose on behalf of America's laudable founding values.

6 | Tolerance, Discrimination, and Discernment

"The general psychology of our people today can be described as spiritless. What manifests itself in behavior is this: lack of discrimination between good and evil, between what is public and what is private, and between what is primary and what is secondary."
— Chiang Kai Shek, Speech, Nanchang 1934

SECULARISM IS BLUSTERY in its words, but is a quiet ideology in its actions. A polemicist might pen a seething attack on the supposed delusion of God, but there is nothing inherent in the secularist mode of thought—unlike in fascism, communism, or, indeed, religious millenarianism —that inspires men to pick up a gun and kill another in the name of his beliefs.

In a way, this lack of positive unction is secularism's chief philosophical problem. Take away the precept of an ethical structure whose genesis and moral authority is external to man, and he is left with a pernicious relativism of his own making or with a cold, all-encompassing scientism unable to give sufficient answers to man's ontological questions.

Religion, moreover, involves others in our day-to-day lives. Either in their theology or in their cohesive effect, or in both, religions forge a sense of community and an altruism of good works. And, of course, religion's claim to divinely revealed truth keeps its followers attached to a common set of ethics. Faith gives a people common purpose.

The closest secularism comes to offering an ethical guide to life is not to offer one at all, at least not a systemic one. In secularism, each human is ultimately his own moral guide. So in our time, "self-actualization" and "reaching one's potential"—which elsewhere in history would have seemed clichés nearly devoid of meaning—have come to represent a significant, if not the most significant, goal of human existence.

The pursuit of self-improvement is an element of the American Dream, make no mistake. In an affluent, free, and liberal society, one has every opportunity to transform himself and to improve his lot in life: A poor man can become rich; an uneducated one, informed; a crass and vulgar one, suave and refined. But what happens when this pursuit takes place in a cultural climate in which almost *any* practice is tolerated?

Consider an example that is, sadly, not as extreme or unusual as it should be.

Many Ivy League student newspapers publish advertisements for egg donors. One recent one read: "Intelligent, Athletic Egg Donor Needed for Loving Family. You must be at least five feet, ten inches, have a 1400-plus SAT score, and possess no major family medical issues." It offered $50,000 remuneration, about ten times what is typically offered to egg donors by fertility registries, to the tall, intelligent, athletic woman who could fit the bill. According to a representative of the couple, the search was reduced to 105 candidates from Yale, Harvard, Princeton, and Stanford, chosen from the more than three hundred women who responded. "This couple wants a baby," a family spokesman

ethnicity, race, and religion in society at large. Just as the person is increasingly programmed and conditioned, so too is society at large.

Despite the almost sacramental use of the word "diversity" in the realm of government and higher education, university life has become a hothouse of intellectual conformity. When my daughter Jaclyn was a first-year student at Northwestern University, she took an introductory politics course, which included once-a-week discussion sections comprised of about fifteen students and a doctoral student who led the meeting. In her discussion group, the graduate instructor shamelessly force-fed the students her opinions on all matters political, usually without offering anything in the way of evidence: "Bush is a liar," or "Republicans are fools," or worse. On one occasion, throwing caution to the wind, my daughter and another young man challenged her contention that the United States is a hopelessly racist society whose class system militates against progress.

Rather than ask the students to expand on their critique and justify their claims, the Ph.D. student replied simply, "You must be Republicans." The young man said, "That has nothing to do with the argument, but I *am* a Republican." As they went on, the instructor admitted, "I stopped listening when you said you were a Republican."

This intolerance is far more deeply entrenched than the lay public probably appreciates. The massive imbalance in political views in higher education has become commonplace. Writing in *The New York Times*, John Tierney pointed to several empirical studies confirming faculty bias. He noted that "a national survey of more than 1000 academics shows that Democratic professors outnumber Republicans by at least seven to one in the humanities and social science. That ratio is more than twice as lopsided as it was three decades ago, and it seems quite likely to keep increasing, because younger faculty members are more consistently Democratic than the ones nearing retirement."

Tierney also called attention to a study of voter registration records at two major universities that included younger academics (assistant and associate professors) sampled from both the hard and social sciences, as well as the humanities. Here, 183 were Democrats, versus 6 Republicans.

The rationalization for this bias among the liberal professors Tierney interviewed was most revealing of all. Many simply regard Republicans as ignorant, driven by religious impulses, or doctrinaire. It rarely occurs to these leftist professors that they are probably more dogmatic than the Republicans they indict.

Yet it is not bias that is so deplorable; it is the transformation of bias into an orthodoxy that cannot countenance another point of view. An academy that once put a premium on the free exchange of ideas has been converted into a breeding ground for intolerance. Should a student, like my daughter, have the temerity to challenge the orthodoxy, silence or rebuke is her reward.

In June 2005, the American Council on Education and twenty-nine institutions of higher education issued a "Statement on Academic Rights and Responsibilities" affirming support for "intellectual pluralism and academic freedom," but insisting that universities, not state legislatures, were the only bodies capable of safeguarding these values. Even with that caveat, it was surprising the ACE would acknowledge a problem it preferred to stay aloof from; apparently, the statement was designed to offset growing concerns about the ideological homogeneity on campuses.

In an effort to capitalize on the ACE statement, the American Council of Trustees and Alumni (ACTA) sent a letter to the signatories as well as to the presidents and chancellors of major universities and colleges requesting information about steps taken to implement the principles enunciated in the statement. None of them reported specific, concrete plans to implement the ACE's outlined vision. "It's all talk and no action," said ACTA president Anne Neal. "Higher education simply can't have it both ways. Colleges and universities presidents say they, alone, are able to correct the situation in the classroom, but then they refuse to do anything but offer lip service to the idea of intellectual diversity. If the Academy were faced with just one study showing racism or sexism in the classroom it would take immediate action to address the problem. Here we see study after study pointing out a breathtaking lack of intellectual diversity on campus and nothing is done about it. The double standard is outrageous."

From a purely pedagogical stance, students at many institutions are shortchanged. Instead of being presented with a variety of perspectives and encouraged to think for themselves, they are often fed an orthodoxy which they must regurgitate for their professorial masters. Not everyone, of course, is complacent about this matter. Todd Zywicki, a Dartmouth College trustee, and Benno Schmidt, chairman of CUNY's trustees, applauded ACTA's efforts. And Judith Richards Hope, a former Harvard Corporation member, charged that "Universities have been aware of the growing lack of intellectual diversity and, for the most part, looked the other way."

It is remarkable that in this land of the free, universities have become islands of soft oppression where students either adhere to prevailing prejudices or face the withering effects of chastisement. A combination of faculty political bias and political correctness has resulted in an academy that resembles an indoctrination center more than an open forum for the free exchange of ideas.

Overlooked at most colleges is that academic freedom is a right granted to professors in a sacred trust that they will not use the classroom as a soapbox for their pet causes and personal politics. Moreover, this freedom comes with a duty to employ competence in an area of study and to rely on reason as the method for the discovery and propagation of knowledge. This, really, is the key to our current troubles. Were the bias in higher education merely political a pas sionate conviction to govern the country in one particular way—it might at least inspire empathy. But today's academic orthodoxy eschews all claims of truth, except those consonant with prevailing academic sentiments.

This was on full display at a school in New York City recently, when a teacher upbraided one of her students for criticizing clitoridectomies, routinely conducted in Africa, explaining that "we should not judge others by our standards." My guess is that this same teacher would not hesitate to upbraid an Evangelical Christian student for advocating prayer in school. Elsewhere, at a large urban university, a discussion led to censure of a middle-class girl who, during her prom, gave birth, and discarded the infant in a dumpster, where it died. The discussion leader asked, "Who are we to judge this young woman? We don't know what was going through her mind." And during debates at the Oakland, California, school board about the introduction of Ebonics, a proponent tellingly argued that "as long as we can respect differences, it doesn't matter what students learn."

These three examples are merely snapshots of tolerance gone mad. Americans today have been told time and again that the opposite of tolerance is intolerance, not rational and informed discernment. When posed with the false dichotomy of tolerance versus intolerance, few educators or members of the public will ally themselves with what is perceived as bigotry. But such a choice favors style over substance. It requires nothing merely to say that one is tolerant. To be tolerant of what is good and worthy, and intolerant of what is ugly and wrong—is the challenge.

Tolerance shouldn't have any room for criminality, though orthodox relativists employ tolerance as a rationalization for almost any behavior. Even throwing a newborn infant in a dumpster—an action almost cartoonish in its illustration of the difference between good and evil—can find second-guessers and defenders.

One's core beliefs are necessarily sacrificed to the logic of tolerance. To criticize customs alien and repellant to a community that has a settled notion of morality is the very definition of modern intolerance. If an orthodox Jew or Catholic accepts the premises of tolerance education, he must forsake his religious convictions on homosexuality and much else.

Despite the prevailing multiculturalism, why shouldn't all societies be valued in the same way? Those that emphasize life, civil liberties, virtue, goodness, and beauty are to be admired over those that promote or condone savagery and barbarism. When Saul Bellow, in his capacity as Nobel laureate, commented, "I will read the Zulus when they have produced a Tolstoy," he was criticized for intolerance. But Bellow was simply applying a standard of discernment. He was arguing that it is important for students to read great works, not a hodgepodge of dubious significance.

If anything, Western secularists seem to show the least regard for their own heritage, even while falling over themselves to excuse others. When caricatures of the prophet Mohammed were printed in the Danish *Jyllands-Posten*, leading to riots around the globe, many U.S. news sources refused to reprint them. Yet American pop culture is fully comfortable ridiculing Christians as extremists and dullards. When something as offensive to Christians as *The Da Vinci Code*, for example, which challenges the basic history and principles of the faith, was launched, protest proved useless. Even after an outcry, particularly among Catholics whose faith was twisted by the novel and the film, the movie's producers refused to include any disclaimer.

America's government, from the federal courthouse to the school board, has become an official enforcer of secularism. Such was Brittney McComb's experience: As her high school's valedictorian, she had her microphone turned off when she mentioned God and Jesus in her commencement address. (Her assigned topic was the inspiration for her superior performance in school; she claimed it was Christianity). It is nearly impossible to erect a nativity scene or post the Ten Commandments on public property anymore, even though this was once commonplace.

Why this double standard? It's simple, really: Western, Judeo-Christian culture is ashamed of itself and in retreat. Secularists would probably bash Islam, too, were it not so quick to react with a violent defense.

But it's high time the most positive elements of our culture reassert themselves—not by violence, but by reason, argumentation, and other manifestations of confidence. "Taboo" has been shunted to the ash heap of history. The word connotes a culturally enforced prohibition, typically heeded to protect one's society, but the concept is all but extinct in America today. Any perversion has defenders, if not *per se* then in principle, as the First Amendment is re-interpreted to include the protection of any kind of expression and action, even those unrelated to speech. The age of consent, incest, and pornography have all found defenders under its aegis.

How has this happened? Surely most people don't approve of eliminating these restrictions. Yet the cultural drift continues. Without judgment, without discrimination, without a sense of right and wrong, taboos cannot exist. Removed from religion's timeless moral injunctions, secularists rely on the multiculturalist tendency to ask, "Who are we to condemn or censure? By what authority can we judge others?"

Os Guinness explains that "naturally no one likes to be charged with racism, colonialism, or chauvinism. Nor does anyone want to be caught 'blaming the victim' or found 'misrepresenting the voice of the voiceless' with standards or categories 'imposed by outside cultures of domination.' But the upshot is a chilling of inquiry. Tough questions go unasked, serious investigations remain unpursued, spurious claims stay unchallenged." It is precisely that chilling of inquiry that colors the crusade for tolerance.

And so community norms have been scaled back, and those eccentricities that were socially permitted have exploded into a diverse array of "lifestyles." James Hitchcock explained this phenomenon as a kind of insurance policy against opprobrium: "There is, in effect, a great conspiracy in America to extend toleration to all forms of questionable behavior as a way of insuring toleration for one's own. . . . Even those who live in accordance with strict moral principles often find it necessary to be publicly tolerant of behavior which they disapprove. There is no worse social stigma than being thought censorious or puritanical."

Community norms once circumscribed how far toleration could be taken. Adopted by an unspoken consensus, norms are premised, implicitly, on the belief that moral education is necessary, and that the whole society, not just one's parents, must lead by example and chaperone itself.

There is sparse influence of community norms in the digital age. Television's debasement is thorough and unrelenting. A recent study by the Parents' Television Council found that vulgar language on television programming had increased by 4 percent on a per-hour basis in two years. This nastiness also pervades the plots. On one episode of "Seinfeld," masturbation was the theme, with its tasteless storyline occurring in an alleged comedy airing at 8:30 P.M.—7:30 in the more socially conservative states in the Central time zone —even though the program was obviously unsuitable viewing for any family but the Borgias.

The American Academy of Pediatrics has suggested that portrayals of sex on television—sex being the theme of some

66 percent of prime-time programming—may contribute to adolescent sexual precocity. Empirical data examining the relationship is tentative and inadequate, but the evidence is still suggestive.

Sex is an exciting and critical part of life, but it is only one part of life. What producers must learn is that their responsibility is not only to a bottom line but also to a public trust. Evidence provided by television researchers suggests that network shows are becoming racier to attract larger audiences.

Raunchiness is also the crux of almost all successful rap music. MTV cheerfully explores the boundaries of acceptable viewing, with partial nudity and simulated scenes of fornication accompanying the latest "songs." Even *The New York Times* had a story about the marriage of rap music and pornography.

Rap icons are symbols of debauchery, violence, and unapologetic prurience. 50 Cent's personal experience, which includes an impressive array of arrests, is incorporated into his lyrics. He is proud to be a "gangsta." Headlines about 50 Cent and his posse being involved in a shooting at a radio station on Manhattan's west side emerged one day before the release of *Massacre*. The incident apparently didn't hurt sales: *Massacre* sold 1.14 million copies in its first four days, the largest total ever reached in an abbreviated sales cycle. Geoff Mayfield, *Billboard*'s director of charts, said, "Rap is the kind of genre where contrary publicity can actually help an album like this." 50 Cent holds the previous record, too, for the suggestively entitled *Get Rich or Die Tryin'*, which sold 872,000 copies in four days.

It is utterly perverse that a shooting incident in which at

least one person was injured could accelerate sales. While studies do not exist demonstrating a causal link between rap and street violence, all one has to do to grasp such a link is listen to the conversation of students outside of any public high school in the United States. Language has grown coarse. Promiscuous sexual behavior is expected. Violence is very much in the air.

Pitirim Sorokin, in his book *Crisis of the Age*, argued that the West had entered into an "advanced sensate age," a period in which sensual pleasures are superordinated over idealistic or ideational values. That was more than fifty years ago. One wonders what Sorokin would say about that same culture today, a milieu that has been so polluted and is so widely disseminated that the average person unknowingly acquiesces in his own degradation. Neil Postman entitled one of his books *Amusing Ourselves to Death*. Yet it isn't amusement that degrades; it is the loss of seriousness—the inability to confront the current reality.

The sensual, which is easy to sell, flushes intelligence and subtlety out of the body-politic. Radio and television executives have a stake in pushing their choices to the very limit, and so create the next big hit. The subject matter of reality television, bad enough in its beginning, has declined; once, its grist was merely staged athletic competitions, tinged with intrigue, but now it concerns itself with the intrigue *per se*.

There isn't a constituency for mass culture's cleansing. Raise the banner of cultural decay and an even taller banner will be raised on behalf of free expression. Discuss taste and a music representative will say: What you consider tasteful is not what I consider tasteful. Moral relativism is a useful club against criticism.

Herbert London

American society experienced a conservative *revanche* after the decadence of the 1960s. Americans had realized by the '70s that things had gotten out of hand. Even the sexual revolution, which ushered in a monolithic change in sexual ethics, failed to achieve the sought-for "liberation" it promised. In communes that promoted free love, partners became resentful, jealous, and distrustful. What started as utopian sexual freedom often ended as old-fashioned sexual tension.

Tolerance is generally a positive thing, but it has run amok in America, and has permitted the degradation of the very culture that values it. To come together, settle moral questions, and create community norms: This is human society's nature. But a society in which tolerance is the highest calling renders each man's judgment a law unto itself. And so the community standard becomes the lowest common denominator of human discernment and taste. This is what ails American culture, and only a sense of community and a sense of right and wrong can save it.

Conclusion

MUCH OF WHAT Americans are and will be as a people was determined by the September 11 terrorist attacks. A nation at war sets new priorities for itself. As Samuel Johnson quipped, nothing concentrates the mind like the prospect of hanging in a fortnight. Self-indulgent fantasies are revealed for what they are, and one wonders why anyone ever paid attention to them in the first place. Although there is no healthy side to war, its ability to purge absurd ideas from public debate can be an ancillary benefit. And there can be no better example of what must be excised from America's body politic than secular humanism, which has shown itself unable to value anything other than the individual, or propose the positive vision necessary to combat our implacable enemies.

A decade ago, Francis Fukuyama wrote *The End of History*, a Hegelian analysis which argued that the close of the Cold War had ushered in the triumph of liberal democracy. The philosophical dialectic that had precipitated nearly fifty years of clashes between East and West was said to be at an end. All nations, or so Fukuyama thought, wanted free markets and a form of constitutional government. The exception of Islamic fundamentalism was regarded by him as a mere historical footnote. Today, alas, this view seems naïvely optimistic.

A decade ago, Samuel Huntington challenged Fukuyama's thesis in a book still worth reading, entitled *The Clash of Civilizations*. Huntington maintained that transcendent philosophical differences could lead to global conflict between Western liberal democracies and radical Islam. Benjamin Netanyahu, Israel's former prime minister, has said "What is at stake today is nothing less than the survival of civilization." So far, this view has proven to be the more unpleasant but also the more realistic one.

On one matter there is no controversy. A substantial portion of the world's people is infected with a virulent hatred of the West. Islamic hatred of the United States is probably more widespread than many experts acknowledge, regardless whether the grievances that inspire such hatred are real or imagined. In a recent poll, 80 percent of Egyptian respondents said that the United States is not *an* enemy, but *the* enemy. The televised images of Palestinians in Gaza and the West Bank rejoicing on September 11 confirmed that this sentiment is widely held in the Islamic world.

One can only hope that the magnitude and enormity of those attacks on America have sunk into the soul of the nation. One hopes as well that in order to reach the end of history, if such a feat is even possible, we will prevail in the clash of civilizations. And one prays that the secularists who preach relativism on our campuses and in our media will realize that Islamism's evil is real, that it is far more oppressive than anything Americans have on offer, and that it threatens us now.

For much of the twentieth century, universities served a public function. Despite a political orientation that tended, systematically, to progressivism and the Left, American higher education cultivated patriotism, a respect for free markets, and a belief in exceptional American traditions. It is no coincidence that college students volunteered in large numbers during both world wars. Indeed, Ivy League students made up a majority of the officer corps when America finally intervened in the Great War. Nor is it any accident that the Office of Strategic Services (the forerunner of the Central Intelligence Agency) was made up almost entirely of Yalies.

Needless to say, this dedication to public service changed when the Vietnam generation arrived. In the 1960s and 1970s, many college students lost confidence in their nation. The cultural relativists who came to dominate the university curriculum in the past quarter-century required American students to "understand" our enemies and to pretend to empathize with them. "Tolerance" became the highest principle, the Golden Calf of campus orthodoxy.

The *Wall Street Journal* editorial page contended that universities' anti-war conditioning changed on September 11. The *Harvard Crimson* published a poll showing that 69 percent of the student body was in favor of military action against those who attacked America. The *Crimson*'s editors even reproached the 38 percent of undergraduates who said that they were unwilling to take part in military action themselves, chiding them for supporting the United States "only as long as they can continue to sit comfortably in Cambridge." Similarly, the *Yale Daily News* asked plaintively, "Will we serve?" One of their staff editorials argued, "We must answer the calling of our time—for if we don't, who will?"

Is it possible that several generations inculcated in moral

obtuseness have finally rebelled? Is it possible that their hearts and minds were not captured by their professoriate, comprised of aging Baby Boomers still immersed in nostalgia for their imaginary Woodstock Nation?

Unfortunately, there is considerable anecdotal evidence to the contrary. There are many voices that militate against those who see America as having a legitimate, moral mission. University of Texas Professor Robert Jensen wrote that the attack "was no more despicable than the massive acts of terrorism ... the U.S. government has committed during my lifetime." At NYU, I have heard a recent graduate say that he was unwilling to defend his country because it "has been something of a bully." Another NYU student, who saw the World Trade Center's twin towers fall, asserted, "This is all America's fault anyway." And at Hunter College, on the other side of Manhattan, a student on a soapbox said that the best response to the terrorist attacks is "fighting American racism."

A flaccid form of tolerance, cloaked in self-doubt, precludes an unequivocal denunciation of this evil. It is hard for someone raised on university banalities to believe that Hamas leader Sheik Hasan Josef can possibly be serious when he says, "We like to grow [Islamic martyrs] from kindergarten through college." Whether America's youth are ready to learn something about their obligations to a free, if imperfect, society; whether they can withstand the orthodoxy of relativism that so many of their faculty members embrace; and whether they can overcome a history of appeasement and fight for what is right: These are all open questions.

History awaits the answers, and history is an impatient master. What is already clear is that the patriotic sentiment that immediately followed September 11 has waned. The war in Iraq has stoked a return to Vietnam-era anti-war sentiments. The Bush administration has been deficient in explaining and reinforcing its appropriately bellicose stance.

For several decades, the United States, wealthy beyond the wildest dreams of the Founders and less threatened by its only real menace, the Soviet Union, indulged the whimsical ideas of various propagandists. Advocates of dubious causes captured the attention of television producers from *60 Minutes* to *20/20*. After September 11, however, many of the issues that inspired these programs seem beside the point, if not utterly irrelevant. Take, for example, the decades-long effort to use the military as a vehicle for social engineering. Women were given a prominent position in battlefield operations; the "don't ask, don't tell" policy became a preoccupation of generals; and the military was asked to assume the role of criminal rehabilitator. Most officers knew that this silliness would exert a debilitating effect, but they allowed themselves to be cowed. Now, with a war on terrorism in full throttle, the desire to make the military "look like America" seems anachronistic. The goal should be to use our military capability to defeat those who terrorize this nation. A myopia on the niceties of domestic politics—protecting Alaska's caribou, for instance, from the depredations of Arctic drilling —likewise seems trivial when oil is so obviously a national defense issue.

Anyone weaned on the free exchange of opinion believes that all views should be considered, even those that might threaten the nation's very existence. Yet when the nation is at war, America's openness may be devastating. There are real consequences for national security and our ability to fight a war abroad when the press regards "the public's right to know" as a principle transcendent above all others, even our self-preservation. A free press once meant a responsible press, but since *The New York Times*'s disclosures about Bush administration security measures, national security in the mind of the media seems less important than the freedom of information.

This brings to the surface the hallowed principles of those who subordinate Americans' collective well-being to Americans' individual rights. In the reflex to defend the latter's many incarnations, it must be asked if Americans can any longer chart their own moral unity, to defeat a foe that is fanatically devoted to an all-encompassing ideology. Can a self-indulgent people fight effectively against a people willing to sacrifice?

Certainly, the United States has a number of advantages that would tempt an observer to predict that the twenty-first century will be, like the twentieth, an American century. The U.S. military is still superior to any other. Even China, which many argue could evolve into a second, more amoral superpower, is decades away from posing a serious threat. And so the rest of the world looks to the United States for answers. Very recently, an American deputy secretary of state said, "Everyone's crisis is America's crisis." Why? Even in the gloomy outlook that suggests America lacks moral authority, there is still the rank acknowledgement that the United States possesses military and financial might. There is no question that the United States has serious global responsibilities as a consequence.

Besides might and money, the United States also has an enviable technological edge. Even anti-Americans in Europe and Asia admire the miracles of modern technology. During a visit to Paris, I listened to Jacques Chirac deliver a speech in which he talked about everything that was wrong with the United States. It is decadent, he said, a terrible place, and Americans do not understand what is going on in world affairs. "But," he allowed, "I greatly admire the advances that the United States has made in the technological realm."

The dynamism that drives the American economy also inheres, to some extent, in the public sphere. American openness to change is truly idiosyncratic. The United States passed a sweeping welfare reform in 1996, even as other Western countries stagnated, weighed down by their welfare societies. When former German chancellor Gerhard Schroeder talked about making Germany's economy more like that of the United States, his party lost in local elections.

Finally, the United States possesses a sense of moral universalism that exists nowhere else and exerts, despite claims to the contrary, a beneficial effect in mooring other states in the traditions of classical liberalism. When one seeks a model of human rights, constitutionalism, rule of law, and property rights, the United States still stands alone. It *is* the model. Not long ago, several Hudson Institute scholars had the opportunity to spend some time in Indonesia, where the new president is very keen on establishing a form of federalism. To what does he look? Not to the regional powers, China and Japan, but to the United States and its Constitution.

These are marks in America's favor, to be sure. But they can all be undermined by a lack of self-confidence in our national values. The United States has suffered a loss of nerve in recent years. We show a growing unwillingness either to recognize or to use our extraordinary military advantage.

Herbert London

The press and politicians betray an obsession with potential casualties, which allows even tinhorn dictators to influence and even dictate American policy. This loss of nerve is significant because if you have a military advantage, but are unwilling to use it, the advantage disappears. Iraq offers a clear proof. After the initial success, our operations were tied down by a caution borne of political considerations. Our reluctance left a vacuum where sectarian unrest festered, in time inaugurating the cycle of violence Iraq is embroiled in today. Not until "the surge"—initiated three years into an anemic, failed policy—were American soldiers taken out of their barracks and put onto the frontlines, where they are presently serving to greatly increased effect.

Looking to affairs at home, it is remarkable how America has risen in the past century. Scarcity is now rare, while it was commonplace in the last century. Our material needs fulfilled, Americans must ask themselves the question the Old Testament poses: "After affluence, what?" Americans are not sure of the answer, but have sought answers that don't interdict their pursuit of pleasure. Joseph Schumpeter once outlined what he considered to be a cultural contradiction of capitalism: that wealth can breed hedonism, which decreases one's ability or will to work and produce further wealth. These days, the wealthy cut a check to the government to provide social-welfare services, but are thus cut off from what used to be their private, often religiously inspired undertaking. The disparity between the rich and poor should not offend us *per se*. It is the lack of social bonds between those classes that constitute the telltale signs of a fractured society.

Undoubtedly, this has been occasioned by the emergence

of the technocratic state, fueled by the delusion that a government with just the right know-how could engineer a perfect society. Today, America's two political parties compete to prescribe solutions to life's eternal problems on the basis of social science and statistics. There are few questions politicians cannot promise to solve. The limitations are ripped away on what "those who know best" may plausibly claim by virtue of their public-policy authority. Herein lies a fifth threat to American greatness, the trend toward "soft totalitarianism," as political philosopher Kenneth Minogue has termed it, where the state begins to manage even the smallest things in life. A shining example is the European Union, with its fixation on *harmonization*, which has led to regulations on everything from the size of lawn mowers to Europeans' diets. For their part, Americans live in an age and nation where even smoking is a great crime, but where much else is ignored. As French political scientist Pierre Manent has pointed out, politics once concerned itself with weightier matters, imbued with moral questions that are today the province of an unelected judiciary.

In America, it is a routine of the Left to deprecate legislators who claim religious inspiration or guidance for legislation they sponsor. This view is almost self-evidently absurd. Why would a legislator's religion—often his framework for moral judgment—have so fundamentally different a purpose as to be wholly taboo in the realm of politics? Yet, many people believe just that, in large measure because they view politics as no longer concerning morality, but public policy exclusively. One can see as much from *What's the Matter with Kansas* and a growing corpus of political tracts that proceed on the smug delusion that a man's paycheck will be, in all cases, more important to him than his moral code. A religious man necessarily believes in a moral order external to man. But politics today operates on the anti-theistic assumption that man is a force of nature unto himself, and that his comfort is therefore the only criterion by which to judge political efficacy.

This suggests the philosophical contradiction common in our era, one inherent in modern liberalism. As defined by Locke, Kant, and most secularists, modern liberalism emphasizes the ideal of individual autonomy—the belief that individuals should be free to do as they choose so long as their actions do not harm others. But, too often, this love of individual freedom causes us to neglect the common good. History has provided ample evidence that human nature can tend toward the callous and evil. Long ago, families arose to enforce a sense of common morality; societies and states then came into the picture, their chief aim to punish, in the name of the whole community, a violation of one citizen's rights by another. A society's rules help create social equilibrium. It is more than the sum of the law books' statutes, however: A society's religious institutions, schools, and voluntary associations all encourage good behavior before the state's coercive action must be called upon. Indeed, Jefferson once argued that the ability to distinguish between good and evil was the main purpose of schooling and education. These same social institutions are threatened by unrestrained autonomy. The tension between socialization and autonomy is at the core of liberalism's dilemma, and how we as a nation mediate that tension will be an essential factor in determining America's future.

As I see it, the way to restore philosophical balance to

American ideology is to reassert the notion of public virtue, once seen as implicit in the Constitution and the Declaration of Independence as a necessary constraint on individual autonomy. The historian Gertrude Himmelfarb has discussed a possible remoralization of American society; I would call this process the reemergence of the enduring beliefs historically associated with our national character. Higher education once provided for the reliable cultural transmission of these values, but university professors today are more likely to be avatars of a culture of adversity than explicators of the great American tradition.

The secularist presumption that government must remain neutral on questions of public morality helps to maintain our present national ambivalence about the necessity of such a renewal. The John Stuart Mill position, that the only purpose for the rightful exercise of government power is to prevent harm to others, prevails. Americans correctly fear an intrusive government that will limit liberty through a demand for conformity, but in emphasizing autonomy, philosophers undermine the moral truths and their consequent constraints that organize life. A democratic republic cannot compel citizens to lead virtuous lives. Nevertheless, even a pluralistic society such as ours can consent to a public philosophy that defines civic purposes based on a shared national tradition. National leaders should not be reluctant to define the common good and consider how it might be pursued.

Today, we face problems both because we live, broadly speaking, in a complex, global world that encourages the intellectually lazy embrace of moral relativism at home; and because our own society's ever widening definition of individual freedom creates a conflict between consciousness and conscience. As the Book of Proverbs maintains, "When there is no vision, a people perish."

We are all dependent on one another for a worthy, sustainable code of moral conduct. This requires experience that is handed down from parent to child, from teacher to student. But keep those words in mind: parent and child, teacher and student—what does contemporary society think of them? For the answer, just look at how ordinary American life is portrayed in the movies.

One critic gushed: "A triumph for this year . . . ranks with the finest movies of the '90s." Another said: "a rich, brilliant and unnerving work—a funny movie that hurts. By far the strongest American film of the year." Yet a third said: "genuinely a thing of beauty." They were talking about the Oscar-winning film *American Beauty*, surely one of the most perverse and cliché-ridden movies ever set to celluloid. *American Beauty*—note the title's lazy sarcasm—is a mosaic of sick and broken lives in what is alleged to be a prototypical suburban American community. The movie's plot concerns two dysfunctional families living next door to each other. In the Burnham house, Dad longs for an affair with his sixteen-year-old daughter's best friend, and Mom, driven by an insatiable desire for career success, is having an affair with the "king" of local real estate. The Fitts live next door. Young Ricky, the son of the household, deals drugs and engages in voyeurism with the young girl in the Burnham household. His mother has lost the ability to communicate; depression dominates her every waking moment. Ricky's father, Colonel Fitts, is a retired Marine and a sadist who routinely beats his son. Colonel Fitts is also a collector of Nazi memorabilia (what else?) and, naturally, a latent homosexual.

In this environment, from which life's joys have been all but removed, the American dystopia of Hollywood's imagination is in full flower. As I watched this propaganda unfold, quietly enduring the hammy overacting of Kevin Spacey and Annette Bening, I wondered what kind of impression it would leave on foreign audiences unfamiliar with American life. They would probably leave the theater thinking that America's suburbs are filled with demented solipsists, that sex dominates the fantasies of every adult male, and that the country fosters unspeakable depravity. This vision of America, of course, relies on the radical critique that emerged in the late 1960s; it reminds me of the ludicrous claim of a youthful radical who said, "You don't know what hell is like till you've lived in Scarsdale."

In an art world where criticism of the bourgeoisie is a substitute for imagination, it's easy to understand why so much praise has been heaped on *American Beauty*. Beneath the hype, however, lies a morally bereft, morose view of America designed to confirm the stereotype that emerged from the overheated 1960s. A director and writer who clearly have the talent to make a splash could have devoted themselves to crafting an affirmative vision of what they believe American life should be, rather than offering a snide portrayal of an imagined dystopia. But they did not, and their laziness is altogether typical of American pop culture.

Despite the freedom American culture enjoys today, and despite the public's often uncritical acceptance of the cultural detritus American artists thrust upon them, it is time to consider the effect such cultural fare has on our body politic, specifically on our ability to defend positive national principles.

Culture matters. Decency, sacrifice, and heroism do not emerge spontaneously, and a great nation cannot retain its greatness while wallowing in a depraved culture. Ultimately, culture is at least as important as politics and economics in maintaining a strong nation, and national leaders, too often reticent to lead in the forums where their power is premised on persuasion rather than fiat, should be saying as much. Today, the public square in the United States is clouded by confusion, misinformation, and misguided assumptions. A secularist agenda permeates so much of American culture —even the language we use—that serious discussion about secularism's implications is difficult. Any criticism of relativism, multiculturalism, or the postmodern outlook is muzzled by accusations of sexism, homophobia, or sheer intolerance. The only attitude that cannot be tolerated is intolerance, and defining an adversary's position as intolerant often ends the discussion.

It was a similarly elitist, anti-democratic agitation that exploited the moral exhaustion of the West in the wake of World War I, and facilitated the rise of the pernicious ideologies of communism and fascism in the subsequent decades. In a curious way, we can see a similar convergence today, in which a Left skeptical of Christianity and the free market shares these antipathies with radical Islam, notwithstanding substantial differences on other matters.

One routinely hears the claim that America is awash with an evangelical Christian fervor. In *American Theocracy: The Peril and Politics of Radical Religion, Oil and Borrowed*

Money in the 21ˢᵗ Century, Kevin Phillips worries about this religiosity's political attachment to the Republican Party. But what Phillips ignores is that religious polarization runs in both directions. Republicans have become more religious because Democrats have become more secular. In the process, Democrats have become at least as self-righteous as the Republicans they oppose.

Jimmy Carter, a man who has made plenty of partisan hay criticizing Republican attachment to religion, made these remarks in an *Atlantic* interview. "I was teaching a Sunday school class two weeks ago," he recalled. "A girl, she was about 16 years old from Panama City, Florida asked me about the differences between Democrats and Republicans. I asked her, 'Are you for peace, or do you want more war?' Then I asked her 'Do you favor government helping the rich or should it seek to help the poorest members of society? Do you want to preserve the environment or do you want to destroy it? . . . I told her that if she answered all of those questions, that she believed in peace, aiding the poor and weak, saving the environment, opposing torture . . . then I told her, 'You should be a Democrat.'" When Carter says he is saddened by the way religion is used for partisan political purposes, one wonders what he can possibly mean.

There are secularists who love America and will sacrifice for it. There are secularists who share some, but not all, of the characteristics I've ascribed to them: apathy, a lack of a moral structure external to themselves, a failure to promote a national vision that can bolster America for the twenty-first century. And there are secularists who will dispute every word of the profile I've drawn. Whatever the case, secularists show a greater reluctance to embrace and fight for positive values than do many of our adversaries. We are engaged in a war that is also a battle of ideas. We have fought such a war before and won, but only after we understood who we were up against, and also defined what we believed.

It is noteworthy that many historians of the twentieth century trace responsibility for barbarism and terrorism to extreme ideologies. The Marxist historian Eric Hobsbawm describes the years between 1914 and 1991 as "an era of religious wars," but argues that "the most militant and bloodthirsty religions were secular ideologies." Paul Johnson, the distinguished conservative historian, blames violence on "the rise of moral relativism, the decline of personal responsibility [and] the repudiation of Judeo-Christian values."

As I see it, the rise of new ideologies and old ideologies dressed as new ones—or the decline of old values—cannot be regarded as causes in their own right. Extremist beliefs such as anti-Semitism, to take a dramatic example, have existed for centuries and have been expressed through conduits as diverse as Catholicism, Nazism, Communism, and Islamism. Both religious and secular institutions, in other words, have at one time or another embraced extremism. Obviously, I do not believe secularism is as extreme as radical Islam. But it is difficult, arguably impossible, to oppose fanaticism without a confident belief in something uplifting, definite, positive, and life-affirming. It is instructive that secularists respond to Islamic extremism as they would to mistreated minorities. For them, Muslims are reacting to oppression. The secularist mentality dwells in guilt about racism, colonialism, and imperialism. It cannot conceive that Islamists might believe exactly what they say—that they intend to resurrect the Islamic caliphate and, to do so, bring down the decadent superpower they regard the United States to be. In refusing to imagine that Islamists might just be beyond the pale of rational decision-making, secularists bind themselves to a delusion that prevents any real comprehension of Islamism and its aims.

It is time the United States begins, once more, to speak a language our adversaries can understand; it may be too much to say America should be sacralized, but at the very least it must recognize and defend its religious heritage. When Pope Benedict delivered his Regensburg lecture in 2006, he was engaged in a two-front war. He was confronting the inclination to violence among Islamists and also attempting to convince his co-religionists of the fight ahead. His challenge still stands. Whether Islam will find the will to reform itself is a looming question of our times, but it is equally important to ask whether Christendom, which has often wanted to sit out the battle, will mobilize the spiritual strength to fight for the greatest and most liberating tradition the world has yet known.

ACKNOWLEDGMENTS

While I must take responsibility for any shortcomings in this book, I wish to acknowledge the help of several people. Darren Russell and Caroline Patton provided indispensable help with research, Sam Karnick for organizing the text, Laddyma Thompson with typing and Stefan Beck and Travis Kavulla for their extraordinary job of editing the text. I also feel privileged to work with the redoubtable Roger Kimball, a brilliant writer and the editor of Encounter Books. None of my work would be possible without the continuing support of my wife Vicki and my children, Stacy, Nancy and Jaclyn. And last, the enduring friendship of Nina Rosenwald and Lawrence Kadish has been a source of inspiration.

INDEX

1984 (Orwell), 18

20/20, 85

3Com, 57

50 Cent, 78

60 Minutes, 85

Ahmadinejad, Mahmoud; on Israel, 9

Allegheny County v. American Civil Liberties Union, 23

Al Qaeda, 7

America Alone (Steyn), 7

American Academy of Pediatrics, 77

American Beauty, 92

American Council on Education, 71

American Council of Trustees and Alumni, 72

American Humanists Association, 32

American Theocracy (Phillips), 95

Amusing Ourselves to Death (Postman), 79

Aquinas, Thomas, 39

Aristotle, 30

Asimov, Isaac, 32

Atlantic Monthly, 95

Auletta, Ken, 56

Bacon, Roger, 39

Bell, Daniel, 53,

Bellah, Robert, 6

Bellow, Saul, 75

Bender, Thomas, 62

Benedict XVI, Pope, 5; lecture at Regensburg, 39, 97

Bening, Annette, 93

Billboard, 78

Bin Laden, Osama, 7

Bloom, Allan, 4

Bologna, Cathedral of, 8

Bond, James, 55

Boorstin, Daniel J., 41; on celebrity, 61

Boyle, Robert, 38

Brand, Elton, 57

Breaking the Spell (Dennett), 33

Browning, Robert, 19

Buller, Arthur Henry Reginald, 25

Burnham, James, 10

Bush, George W., 13, 64, 70, 85, 86

Byrne, Rhonda, 15

Camus, Albert, 30

Carter, Jimmy, 95

Catholic Church, 37–38,

Catholicism, 5

Chemical Bank, 56

Chesterton, G.K., 30

Chirac, Jacques, 87

City University of New York, 72

Clash of Civilizations, The (Huntington), 82

Clinton, Bill, 56

Closing of the American Mind, The (Bloom), 4

Index

CMGI Inc., 57
Cold War, 7, 81
Common Sense (Paine), 42
Communism, 10, 66, 96; after World War I, 94;
Conseco, 57
Crisis of the Age (Sorokin), 79

Dartmouth College, 72
Darwin, Charles, 35
Da Vinci Code, The (Brown), 73
Dawkins, Richard, 34
Decalogue, 26, 29
Democracy in America (Tocqueville), 53
Descartes, Rene, 38, 41
Disney Corporation, 56
Dollar, David, 43
Dollar-Kraay Study, 43–45
Dostoevsky, Fyodor, 30

Egypt, 7, 82,
Einstein, Albert, 33, 36
Eisenhower, Dwight, 6
End of History, The (Fukuyama), 81–82
Enron, 57
Erasmus, 6

Fifth Amendment, 49
Fleming, Ian, 55
Forbes magazine, 56
Forum magazine, 33
Frost, Robert, 1
Fruit of the Loom, 57
Fukuyama, Francis, 81–82

Galileo, 37
Get Rich or Die Tryin', 78

Gingrich, Newt, 56
God is Not Great (Hitchens), 26, 40
Gödel, Kurt, 35
Gould, Stephen Jay, 34
Great Satan, 7
Grosseteste, Robert, 40
Guinness, Os, 76
Guttman, Amy, 62

Hamas, 84
Harvard Corporation, 72
Harvard Crimson, 83
Hauser, Marc, 28
Heisenberg, Werner, 35, 41
Hezbollah, 7
Hilton, Paris, 61–62
Himmelfarb, Gertrude, 91
Hitchcock, James, 24, 31, 77
Hitchens, Christopher, 26, 29, 30, 31, 40
Hitler, Adolf, 9
Hobbes, Thomas, 49, 58,
Hobsbawn, Eric, 96
Holland; Amsterdam, 8; Theo van Gogh, murder of, 8
Hope, Judith Richards, 72–73
Huntington, Samuel, 82

Incompleteness Theorem (Gödel), 35
Israel, 7, 8, 9, 82

Jefferson, Thomas, 90
Jensen, Robert, 84
John Paul II, Pope, 47
Johnson, Lyndon, 17, 55
Johnson, Paul, 96
Johnson, Samuel, 81

Index

Josef, Sheik Hasan, 84

Jyllands-Posten, 8, 75

Kaine, Tim, 14
Kaishek, Chiang, 66
Kant, Immanuel, 30, 63, 90
Karl, George, 57
Kelo v. City of New London, 45, 49–51
Kennedy, John F., 17
Kepler, Johannes, 38
Kipling, Rudyard, 11
King Jr., Martin Luther, 17
Kirk, Russell, 32, 42
Kraay, Aart, 43

von Leibniz, Gottfried, 41
Lennon, John, 20
Lewis, Bernard, 6
Lincoln, Abraham, 32
Lindsay, Brink, 29
Locke, John, 48, 58, 90
Lohan, Lindsay, 61

Mamas and the Papas, The, 17
Manent, Pierre, 89
Martel, Charles, 7
Marx, Karl, 46
Marxism, 8, 36
Massacre (50 Cent), 78
Maslow, Abraham, 20, 54
Mayfield, Geoff, 78
McComb, Brittney, 75
Mill, John Stuart, 63, 91
Miller, Perry, 5
Minogue, Kenneth, 89
Modern Physics and Ancient Faith (Barr), 34
Mohammed, cartoons 8, 75; *Divine*

Comedy, 8; frescoes, 8
Moral Freedom (Wolfe), 26–28
Moral Minds (Hauser), 28
MTV (Music Television), 78

Nasrallah, Sheik, 7
Nation Among Nations: America's Place in World History (Bender), 62
National Enquirer magazine, 62
Natural law, 12, 25, 29, 35, 36,
Nazi, 93; Nazism, 96
Neal, Anne, 72
Netanyahu, Benjamin, 82
Neuhaus, Father Richard, 11
New London Development Corp., 50
Newton, Isaac, 38
New York Times, The, 70, 78, 86
Nietzsche, Friedrich, 27

O'Connor, Sandra Day, 50
Office of Strategic Services, 83
On the Genealogy of Morals (Nietzsche), 27
Origin of Species (Darwin), 34
Orwell, George, 3, 50; *1984*, 18

Paine, Thomas, 36–37, 53
Parents' Television Council, 77
Pascal, Blaise, 38
Phillips, Kevin, 95
Pledge of Allegiance, 60
Podhoretz, Norman, 7
Politics of Prudence (Kirk), 32
Postman, Neal, 79
Putnam, Robert D., 53
PSI Net, 57

Index

Rand, Ayn, 16
Reagan, Ronald, 23
Regensburg, University, 39, 97
Reliance Insurance Group, 56
Religious Right, 11
Ritalin, 69
Roepke, Wilhelm, 18
Rousseau, Jean-Jacques, 6, 15–16
Rubin, Jerry, 18
Russell, Bertrand, 35–36

Saladin, 8
Schiavo, Teresa, 12–13
Schmidt, Benno, 72
Schroeder, Gerard, 87
Schumpeter, Joseph, 88
Secret, The, 15
Sennett, Richard,
Shakur, Tupac, 62
Sorokin, Pitirim, 65, 79
Smith, Adam, 19
Snow, C.P., 68
Spacey, Kevin, 93
Stark, Rodney, 38–39
Steinberg, Saul, 56
Stevens, John Paul, 50
Stevenson, Adlai, 50
Steyn, Mark, 7
Summa Theologica, 39
Supreme Court, U.S., 14, 23,

Theory of Moral Sentiments
    (Smith), 19
Tierney, John, 70–71
Tocqueville, Alexis de, 22; on

Christianity in America, 53,
    64–65
Tours, Battle of, 7
Toynbee, Arnold, 19, 65
Trans World Airlines, 57

United Nations, 10, 44; Human
    Rights Council, 63–64

Van Gogh, Theo, 8
Vietnam; war, 17, 59; era, 82, 85

Wall Street Journal, The, 83
Warhol, Andy, 61
Waugh, Evelyn, 20
Wealth of Nations (Smith), 19
What Is Secular Humanism
    (Hitchcock), 24
What's the Matter with Kansas
    (Thomas), 89
Wilson, James Q., 28
Wolfe, Alan, 29
World Bank, 43
World Basketball Championships,
    57
World Trade Center, 84
World Trade Organization, 42
World War I, 94
World War II, 59, 68

Yale Daily News, 83
Yeats, W.B., 3, 10

Zakri, Mustafa, 7
Zywicki, Todd, 72

AMERICA'S SECULAR CHALLENGE has been set in Adobe Systems' Warnock Pro, an OpenType font designed in 1997 by Robert Slimbach. Named for John Warnock, one of Adobe's co-founders, the roman was originally intended for its namesake's personal use, but was later developed into a comprehensive family of types. Although the type is based firmly in Slimbach's calligraphic work, the completed family makes abundant use of the refinements attainable via digitization. With its range of optical sizes, Warnock Pro is elegant in display settings, warm and readable at text sizes — a classical design with contemporary adaptability.

SERIES DESIGN BY CARL W. SCARBROUGH